Soul Mending

HEALING THE ROOT OF FEAR AND TRAUMA

LORENA ROSSI

Soul Mending™ Publishing

Copyright © 2023 by Lorena Rossi
All rights reserved. No part of this book may be used or reproduced in any manner whatsoever without written permission except in the case of brief quotations in the context of critical articles or reviews.

ISBN (Paperback): 978-1-7390708-0-9
ISBN (eBook): 978-1-7390708-1-6

For information: Soul Mending Publishing, soulmending.ca

Cover design by Lorena Rossi
Interior design by Aaxel Author Services

This book is presented solely for educational and entertainment purposes. The author is not offering it as professional services advice. While best efforts have been used in preparing this book, the author makes no representations or warranties of any kind and assumes no liabilities of any kind with respect to the accuracy or completeness of the contents and specifically disclaim any implied warranties of fitness of use for a particular purpose. The author shall not be held liable or responsible to any person or entity with respect to any loss or incidental or consequential damages caused, or alleged to have been caused, directly or indirectly, by the information contained herein. Individuals should seek the services of a competent professional.

Printed in the United States of America

This book is dedicated to all the lost souls finding their way back home.

Acknowledgements

Finding the right words to express my deep gratitude to everyone who has been part of my journey feels overwhelming yet incredibly important. Each person I've crossed paths with has made a lasting impact on my life, and I am forever grateful for their presence.

First and foremost, I want to acknowledge my husband, who has been my rock and source of support throughout this entire journey. When I felt like giving up, he stood by my side, reminding me of who I truly am. His belief in me has given me the strength to keep moving forward.

To my amazing children, words can't fully express how grateful I am for each of you. You have taught me the true meaning of love. Through your laughter, tears, and unconditional affection, you've shown me a love that is deep and limitless. You bring immense joy and purpose to my life, and your beautiful spirits inspire my faith in humanity.

I also want to express my deepest appreciation to my family. My parents and sister have always shown me unwavering love and acceptance, which has given me strength. Their presence has shaped me into the person I am today, and for that, I am deeply grateful. To my guardian angel, my beloved brother in heaven, you have guided me from the beginning of my healing journey. Your presence has been a comforting force, and I find comfort in knowing you watch over me with love.

To every person I've encountered on my journey, even briefly, your presence has contributed to my growth. Our interactions, conversations, and shared experiences have shaped my path in profound ways. Your words of encouragement, kindness, and support have been immensely valuable and have played a significant role in my life.

I want to express my heartfelt thanks to the universe, higher powers, and my entire spiritual team. Your messages, subtle signs and synchronicities have reassured me and reminded me that I'm always supported, especially during difficult times.

A special thank you goes to Archangel Michael, who has been a constant presence and guide throughout my journey. From the very beginning, he has provided support and protection, and without him, Soul Mending wouldn't exist. Archangel Michael, your love, and strength have been a guiding light in my life, helping me face my fears and step into my power. Your unwavering commitment to my well-being has given me courage.

I also want to express my deep gratitude to Elena, a dear friend, teacher, and mentor. I wouldn't be where I am today without your guidance and support. Your presence radiates love and light, not just in my life, but in the lives of many others. Thank you from the bottom of my heart!

Though words may not fully capture the depth of my gratitude, I hope these heartfelt expressions convey a fraction of the immense appreciation I hold. Each of you has played a crucial role in shaping my journey, and I am forever grateful for your presence, love, and unwavering belief in me.

Table of Contents

Chapter 1
Introduction ... 1

Chapter 2
Fragmentation ... 43

Chapter 3
Meet Your Soul ... 57

Chapter 4
Introduction to Soul Mending ... 67

Chapter 5
Before You Begin ... 69

Chapter 6
Diving into Soul Mending ... 81

Chapter 7
Step One - Starting Point and Identifying Your Fears ... 89

Chapter 8
Step Two - The Discovery: Love and Making Contact ... 103

Chapter 9
Step Three - Going Home ... 111

Chapter 10
Step Four - Forgiveness ... 119

Chapter 11
Step Five - Gratitude ... 131

Chapter 12
The Summary ... 135

Chapter 1

Introduction

Trauma can have a profound impact on our lives, affecting our thoughts, emotions, and behaviors, often leading to feelings of disconnection, depression, and anxiety. However, it's important to remember that healing is possible, liberating you from the repetitive patterns they have woven. Soul Mending presents a transformative journey that leads to serenity, happiness, and a harmonious existence. It offers you the opportunity to break free from the shackles of the past, embrace healing, and embark on a path of inner peace and joyful living.

Soul Mending is a transformative journey of healing and self-discovery that guides you to explore the depths of your being, reconnect with your authentic self, and restore the harmony that trauma may have disrupted. By honoring the wisdom of your soul, this journey leads you toward a state of wholeness.

In my personal journey for healing, I encountered a

profound sense of loss, disconnection, and unhappiness stemming from the traumas of my childhood and the devastating event of losing my brother in a tragic car accident. This experience shattered a significant part of my soul, leaving me in a state of profound despair. However, I made a deliberate and courageous choice to change the trajectory of my life by embarking on a journey of self-exploration and seeking a deeper understanding of myself and my experiences.

Inspired by my own experiences and with the support of my spiritual team, I created Soul Mending as an empowering self-healing process. Embracing the practice of Soul Mending brought about profound transformations, not only within myself but also in the lives of my clients. The heavy burden of trauma gradually lifted, enabling us to rediscover our true essence and experience a newfound sense of lightness and clarity. Through the healing process, we reclaimed our inner strength and authenticity, paving the way for personal growth and a renewed outlook on life. The power of Soul Mending allowed us to release the shackles of the past and embark on a journey of healing and self-discovery, ultimately leading us towards greater joy, peace, and fulfillment.

Soul Mending became a powerful tool in my journey of self-discovery and healing, providing me with the means to release the burdens that had held me back for far too long. Through this process, I rediscovered the essence of who I truly am, unburdened by the weight of past experiences. The clarity I gained allowed me to approach life with a renewed perspective, free from the limitations that trauma had imposed upon me.

Soul Mending offers a unique and transformative approach to healing, rooted in personal experience and supported by spiritual guidance. It enables individuals to navigate their own healing journey, unraveling the layers of trauma and reconnecting with their true selves. Through Soul Mending, you too can experience remarkable changes by shedding the heavy burdens of the past and embracing a life of lightness and clarity.

Trauma has the power to fragment our soul, causing parts of our authentic self to disconnect as a survival mechanism. However, as these fragments depart, we lose our power and vitality, often leading to depression and anxiety. In Soul Mending, we will explore the nature of trauma and its effects on our mind, body, and soul.

It is crucial to acknowledge that we are not solely physical beings; we are energetic beings as well. Trauma deeply affects our soul and energy. Therefore, we must approach our healing journey from an energetic perspective. We will delve into the energy of fear, understanding its presence and its impact on our entire energetic system.

Through the process of Soul Mending, we will compassionately reclaim those lost fragments of ourselves, restoring balance and embracing our true power. This journey is one of self-love, self-discovery, and empowerment, allowing us to step into the fullness of our being and live an authentic life filled with joy.

Each step of Soul Mending is an opportunity to embrace our inner strength, wisdom, and resilience. We will uncover the layers of our being, shedding light on hidden aspects and revealing our true essence. By reconnecting with our authentic self, we tap into our innate power and vitality, enabling us to live a purposeful and fulfilling life.

Soul Mending is not a quick fix, but rather a transformative journey that requires dedication, self-reflection, and the courage to confront our inner wounds. Throughout this transformative process, you will embark on a profound journey of self-discovery, unearthing and illuminating the aspects of yourself that have long been forgotten or neglected, residing in the depths of your being. As you courageously delve into the shadows, you will shine a compassionate light on these forgotten parts, offering them the healing and attention they deserve. With each fragment that is acknowledged and embraced, you will experience a profound sense of integration and wholeness, bringing profound healing and transformation to your entire being. The reunion with these lost parts of yourself is a sacred and empowering act, as you reclaim your true essence and nurture the profound connection with your own soul.

At the core of the Soul Mending process is the recognition that healing is not a linear or one-size-fits-all journey. It is a deeply personal and individualized experience that requires patience, self-compassion, and a willingness to delve into the depths of one's being. The steps of Soul Mending serve as guiding principles, offering structure and direction, while also leaving room for intuition and personal interpretation.

Moreover, the Soul Mending journey is not a straightforward or comfortable one. It demands personal accountability and deep introspection. It will challenge you to shift from a victim mentality to a place of self-empowerment, where genuine healing can take place. This process may be uncomfortable and even painful at times, but it is an essential part of the journey toward true healing.

As you embark on this soulful journey of self-discovery, open yourself to the boundless potential for growth and transformation. Soul Mending presents us with a remarkable opportunity to heal, integrate, and reclaim the fragmented parts of our being, thereby paving the way for an authentic and wholehearted life brimming with profound joy. Let us honor ourselves by wholeheartedly embracing this empowering leap towards a future filled with hope and endless possibilities.

What Is Trauma?

Trauma is a big and complex word that carries significant weight and implications. It refers to deeply distressing or disturbing experiences that overwhelm an individual's ability to cope or integrate the emotions associated with those experiences. Traumatic events can range from singular incidents, such as accidents or natural disasters, to ongoing situations like abuse or prolonged exposure to violence.

One reason why people may struggle to recognize or acknowledge their own experiences as trauma is because trauma manifests differently in everyone. The impact of trauma can be influenced by various factors, including personal resilience, support systems, and coping mechanisms. Additionally, societal norms, cultural beliefs, and the way trauma is portrayed in media can shape our understanding and recognition of traumatic experiences.

Another factor that contributes to the difficulty in acknowledging personal trauma is the tendency to compare our experiences to what we perceive as "extreme" or "obvious" traumas. Society often associates trauma with severe or life-threatening events, leading individuals to dismiss or minimize their own experiences if they do not match those extreme criteria. However, it is important to remember that trauma is subjective and deeply personal. What may be traumatic for one person may not be for another.

Trauma can often be subtle or hidden, meaning that its impact may not be immediately apparent or easily recognized. Traumatic events can leave deep emotional wounds that may be buried beneath the surface, making them less visible or noticeable to others and even to the person who has experienced the trauma. This can happen for various reasons, such as the individual's coping mechanisms, the passage of time, or the complexity of the traumatic memories. The subtle or hidden nature of trauma highlights the importance of recognizing and addressing its impact, even when it may not be readily apparent, to promote healing and well-being.

Traumatic experiences can become buried in the subconscious mind as a self-protective mechanism, making it challenging to access and process those memories. This can result in individuals feeling disconnected from their own traumatic experiences or struggling to understand the impact those experiences have had on their lives.

It is crucial to create a safe and supportive environment that encourages open dialogue and validates the experiences of trauma survivors. By fostering understanding, empathy, and education about trauma, we can help individuals recognize and acknowledge their own experiences. It is important to remember that everyone's journey is unique, and each person's healing process will unfold in its own time and way.

Ultimately, acknowledging and validating our own experiences of trauma is a significant step towards healing and reclaiming our personal power. It is essential to honor our stories, emotions, and individual journeys as we work

INTRODUCTION

towards healing and building resilience in the face of trauma.

Trauma, at its core, is the emotional aftermath that arises from experiencing a distressing and overpowering event or circumstance. It goes beyond the immediate impact of the incident and deeply affects your emotional well-being and sense of safety in the world. Traumatic experiences can leave lasting imprints on your psyche, influencing your thoughts, emotions, and behaviors long after the event has passed.

There are three primary types of traumas: acute, chronic, and complex. Acute trauma refers to a single specific event, such as a car accident, the loss of a loved one, job loss, divorce, miscarriage, or a near-death experience. Chronic trauma involves living in an environment that is physically, emotionally, psychologically, or spiritually unsafe over an extended period. Complex trauma is a combination of acute and chronic trauma, which is often the experience of most individuals throughout their lives.

When we encounter any form of trauma, whether acute, chronic, or complex, our instinctual response is to enter survival mode. This mode triggers the release of stress hormones, activating the fight, flight, or freeze response. In survival mode, our mind and body become hyper focused on defending against potential dangers, even when those dangers are not rational.

A rational fear is a natural and understandable response to a real threat or danger. It is a fear that matches the level of risk in a specific situation. For example, being afraid of a dangerous animal or feeling fear when standing at a great height are rational fears. These fears help protect us by making us aware of potential harm and prompting us to take necessary precautions or avoid the danger altogether. Rational fears are rooted in our instinct to stay safe and are often based on clear and identifiable dangers in our surroundings.

Unlike irrational fears, which are excessive and don't match the actual risk, rational fears have a purpose and can keep us out of harm's way in potentially risky situations. An irrational fear is when someone feels an intense and ongoing fear of something specific, like an object, situation, or activity. This fear is much stronger than what is reasonable or necessary, and it can cause a lot of distress. An example of an irrational emotional fear is being extremely afraid of public speaking. While it's normal to feel some nervousness or anxiety when speaking in front of an audience, an irrational fear of public speaking goes beyond typical apprehension and can cause a lot of distress and avoidance behavior. This fear can be much greater than the actual threat and may lead to panic attacks, sweating, trembling, or a strong desire to get away from the situation. The fear can continue even when there's no real danger to a person's safety or well-being. They may fear negative judgment, humiliation, or embarrassment, even though the actual consequences of public speaking are usually not that severe.

Fear is a powerful energy that arises from the pain and distress caused by traumatic experiences. To better understand this concept, let's explore a visual representation of the layers involved in a wound.

At times, we find ourselves fearing the re-experience of the pain we initially felt during our traumatic events. As a result, we tend to avoid situations or stimuli that remind us of those painful moments. However, it's important to rec-

INTRODUCTION

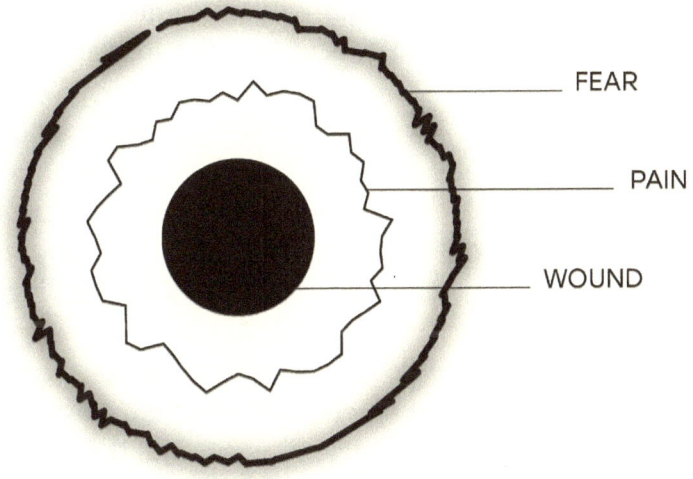

Energetic Imprint of Trauma

ognize that we often encounter triggers in our daily lives, causing our wounds to resurface. This triggers the pain we carry within us, leading us to fear facing and feeling that pain once again. This creates an ongoing cycle of avoidance and fear.

When we encounter triggers, they act as reminders of our past traumas and activate the emotions and sensations associated with those experiences. Our natural response is to protect ourselves by avoiding or suppressing these triggers to prevent the resurfacing of painful memories. However, this cycle of avoidance and fear can hinder our healing process.

It's important to acknowledge that while it may be uncomfortable, allowing ourselves to feel and explore the pain associated with our wounds is an essential part of the healing journey. By confronting our fears and leaning into the discomfort, we create an opportunity for healing and growth.

Breaking the cycle requires us to develop a compassionate and understanding relationship with ourselves. It involves gradually building resilience and the ability to navigate through triggering moments. By consciously engaging with our wounds and the emotions they evoke, we begin to unravel the cycle of fear. It allows us to gain a deeper understanding of ourselves, process the unresolved emotions, and gradually release the grip that fear has on us. Through this process, we can cultivate resilience, inner strength, and a sense of empowerment as we continue on the path of healing and growth.

INTRODUCTION

Trauma's Effects on Our Body and Mind

Trauma is not only confined to our minds; it is stored within our bodies, specifically in the psoas muscle (pronounced so-as). Often referred to as the "Muscle of the Soul," the psoas holds the cellular imprints of traumatic events and experiences. It acts as a storage space, preserving these wounds until they are healed.

The psoas muscle consists of two muscles, but it is often regarded as a single large muscle. It is in the pelvic region and extends upward on either side of the lower and mid back, connecting our torso to our legs. It is also linked to a vital part of our brain known as the reptilian brain, responsible for our primal instincts. The psoas muscle retains our survival impulses and can influence our fight, flight, or freeze response.

Connected to the psoas muscle is a nerve that runs along our spine called the Vagus nerve. This nerve plays a role in our digestion, heart rate, and immune system. Trauma can disrupt the functioning of the Vagus nerve, leading to dysfunction throughout the body. Information travels up this nerve and reaches a part of the brain that signals potential danger.

Over the years, during my private sessions with clients, I have observed this sequence of triggered trauma in the psoas, the transmission of signals via the Vagus nerve, and the delivery of information to the brain. I received this information through reading their energy and using my clairvoyance. However, I didn't fully understand its meaning at the time. I would observe trauma at the base of their spine and a signal traveling upward, resembling a thin wire transmitting information to a specific area of their brain.

I noticed that most clients consistently lived in this state, meaning that they were in survival mode for most of their existence. This meant their bodies rarely entered a state of rest and digestion.

When we are unable to achieve a state of rest and digestion, our bodies remain tense, and our nervous system becomes dysregulated. This leads to increased irritability, easy triggers, anxiety, depression, and constant overthinking. The mind goes into overdrive, tirelessly analyzing situations like a hamster wheel constantly spinning. It now governs our lives, influenced by past traumas, hindering our ability to perceive situations objectively with clarity and discernment. Living in this perpetual state of fight, flight, or freeze mode can be mentally, emotionally, physically, and spiritually draining.

Each day, we possess a finite amount of energy that can be expended. However, when we are in survival mode, most of our energy reserves are depleted just to navigate through the day and ensure our survival. There is little time and energy left for flourishing, creating, and exploring. The opportunity to relax, surrender, and embrace the present moment becomes a luxury we cannot afford.

Surrendering requires acceptance, trust, and vulnerability. Yet, how can one trust the world and allow oneself to be vulnerable when there are countless threats to their well-being? How can you accept your present circumstances when they cause immense pain and discomfort? Your body and mind instinctively resist surrender and lowering your defenses to shield you from physical and emotional pain. They work tirelessly to avoid potential experiences that may trigger old traumas, as the memories of these traumas are stored within the body, particularly in the psoas muscles. If you find it challenging to be fully present in the moment, it is important to be kind to yourself and understand that surrender is a gradual process. Instead, surrender to your current reality, acknowledging your truth and accepting where you are. Surrendering begins with embracing your present circumstances instead of fixating on where you believe you should be.

Trauma's Effects on Our Soul

Trauma not only impacts our body and mind but also has profound effects on our soul, the essence of our being. Our body serves as a vessel, a home for our soul and the conscious awareness of our existence. When we experience trauma, a part of our soul instinctively withdraws from its vessel, detaching itself from the conscious self to avoid the pain and memories associated with the event. This detachment may lead to forgetting childhood memories or feeling disconnected from our emotions.

Regardless of the type or severity of the traumatic event, the part of our soul that experiences the pain departs from the body and mind. In my private sessions with clients, I have witnessed fragmented souls stuck in the time of the event, disconnected from the conscious self, leaving the body and mind. Often, clients are unaware of these missing fragments. What they experience are the symptoms of the fragmented soul, ranging from anxiety and depression to disconnection and a lack of joy in their lives.

From the moment we are born until the present moment, fragments of our soul have been lost along the way. Each traumatic event chips away at our soul, weakening or breaking pieces off. Over time, these pieces become lost and disconnected from our body and mind. Visualize holding a vase in your hands, with each blow representing a traumatic event. Each blow either creates a crack, weakening the vase, or breaks off a piece. Gradually, the vase loses its pieces until it is unrecognizable. However, these pieces have not disappeared; they are lost. The beautiful aspect is that we can gather and put these pieces back together, just like the ancient Japanese practice of kintsugi, where broken ceramics are repaired using gold, making the object stronger and more beautiful than before.

Our soul is like that precious vase, and our body and mind serve as the hands that mend it. Our soul possesses a unique shape, but each traumatic event fractures a piece away from our body and mind. In psychology, we refer to this as dissociation, while in spirituality, it is known as soul fragmentation. Soul fragmentation can make us feel disconnected, empty, and lost, leaving us with a sense of powerlessness.

The loss of personal power impacts our boundaries, confidence, self-esteem, ability to act, and inner strength. When personal power is lacking, we seek it externally, reaching for things like food, alcohol, sex, social media, and even other people to fill the void. However, this only serves to diminish our power further, making us weaker and more vulnerable to future traumas.

There is a saying, "it's what broke the camel's back," indicating that one final blow can be the breaking point for the soul. The last significant piece shatters, leaving us no choice but to pause and embark on the healing journey because moving forward becomes untenable. Healing does not imply that we won't face new challenges or traumas in life, but it equips us with strength, resilience, and greater preparedness to navigate through these experiences.

We are a combination of body, mind, and soul, and it is crucial to address the healing of our soul alongside our body and mind. We must approach healing from a holistic perspective, recognizing that the well-being of our soul greatly impacts the rest. Soul Mending is a transformative process that focuses on the healing of the soul, helping us find and reclaim the lost fragments, enabling us to mend ourselves in a profound and enduring manner. It is an invitation back to wholeness, where the integration of body, mind, and soul can truly occur.

Our Chakra System and How Trauma Affects It

The chakra system, derived from the Sanskrit word meaning "wheel," refers to the energy points in our body. These spinning energy centers are intended to remain open and aligned. Each chakra corresponds to specific sets of nerves, major organs, and areas of our energetic body, influencing our emotional and physical well-being. The chakra system consists of seven main energy centers located in specific areas of our body, through which life force energy flows. Life force energy, also known as Chi, is the energy that permeates our body and connects us to all living things, such as trees, flowers, animals, the ocean, and the sky. It represents the harmonious balance between Yin, the feminine energy, and Yang, the masculine energy. We will delve deeper into the meanings of feminine and masculine energy later in the book, but for now, let's explore each chakra, its role in our overall health, the associated elements, the colors represented by each chakra, and how trauma affects the chakra system.

Why are we examining our chakra system? Trauma impacts us energetically before it manifests physically. As energetic beings composed of vibrating particles and atoms, we cannot overlook the effects of trauma on our energetic system, commonly known as the chakra system. Taking a holistic approach to healing, which encompasses the body, mind, and soul, requires us to consider the well-being of our chakra system.

Each chakra is distinct, associated with an element and a color. The elements associated with the chakras are earth, water, fire, air, and ether. The seven colors corresponding to the chakras are red, orange, yellow, green, blue, indigo, and violet. Each element and color carry a unique frequency, and you will discover why they are intricately linked to each chakra. The state of our chakra system directly impacts our physical and mental health, thus influencing both our body and mind.

Chakra #1 — Root

The Root chakra, also known as the first chakra, is situated at the base of the spine. It encompasses and influences various parts of our physical body, including the spine, lower back, legs, feet, immune system, and skin. As we have previously explored, trauma can become lodged in the psoas muscle, which aligns with the location of the root chakra. This connection implies that the root chakra can carry the energetic imprints of traumatic experiences due to its association with the psoas muscle.

The psoas muscle, a deep core muscle that runs along the lumbar spine and connects to the pelvis and legs, plays

INTRODUCTION

Root Chakra

a vital role in our fight-or-flight response. It contracts when we perceive danger or experience stress, preparing our body for action. Since trauma can activate this response, the psoas muscle may become tense and chronically contracted, holding onto the energetic residue of traumatic events. Consequently, this tension and energetic imprint can impact the functioning of the root chakra.

The root chakra is primarily associated with our sense of safety, security, and stability. It is responsible for grounding us in the physical world and establishing a solid foundation for our lives. When trauma is stored in the psoas muscle and influences the root chakra, it can disrupt our ability to feel secure and stable, leading to imbalances in this energetic center. These imbalances may manifest as physical symptoms, such as lower back pain, issues with the legs or feet, compromised immune function, or even skin conditions.

Healing and restoring balance to the root chakra involve addressing the stored trauma in the psoas muscle and releasing its energetic imprints. In the process of Soul Mending, individuals can gradually release the energetic imprints of trauma, restore balance to their system, and foster a greater sense of well-being, resilience, and inner harmony. By addressing and resolving the trauma held in the root chakra and the psoas muscle, we can support the reestablishment of a strong foundation, a sense of safety, and a greater connection to the authentic self.

The energy associated with trauma that remains in the root chakra is fear. Fear has a low vibrational frequency and is dense in nature, much like the element earth, which is associated with the root chakra. Red is also linked to the root chakra and carries the lowest frequency among all the colors.

INTRODUCTION

Being the first chakra, the root chakra serves as the foundation for the entire chakra system. Just as any structure relies on a solid foundation, what we build upon it depends on the stability and strength of that foundation. The root chakra develops during early childhood, particularly between the ages of 0 and 7 when our personal foundation is being established.

A healthy foundation is established in an environment that is emotionally, physically, psychologically, and spiritually safe. However, whether we experience a single traumatic event or prolonged exposure to an unsafe environment during early childhood, our root chakra can be compromised. Although each chakra functions independently, they significantly influence one another. When the root chakra is compromised, the entire system needs to compensate and adjust to maintain balance.

Since the root chakra forms our foundation and we recognize the importance of a solid foundation for a healthy system, it is crucial to explore the fears present in our root chakra, understand their roots, and ultimately learn how to release them. Soul Mending provides a framework to guide you through these steps in a simple and accessible manner. By addressing and healing the root chakra, you can establish a solid foundation for overall well-being and growth.

Like caring for a garden, you cannot force a plant to grow; it grows on its own. Your role is to nurture the soil, to the earth itself. Remove any weeds that hinder the plant's growth, water the soil, and provide it with essential nutrients and vitamins. By tending to the soil, the plant will thrive and become healthy and robust. In the same way, direct your attention to your root chakra, which represents the earth element. Clear and nurture your root chakra by healing past traumas and releasing fear. As a result, you will naturally experience growth, expansion, and flourishing in your life.

Chakra #2 – Sacral

Moving up to the second chakra, the Sacral chakra, it is located below the navel and governs the kidneys, spleen, gallbladder, ovaries, blood, and bladder. The element associated with the sacral chakra is water, and its color is orange. This chakra is responsible for emotions, the subconscious mind, creativity, sensuality, and sexuality. It develops between the ages of 7 and 12, when we start to form a sense of self and establish our identity. Our sense of self encompasses our personality traits, skills, preferences, belief system, values, moral code, and the things that bring us joy in life. It shapes our self-image and identity.

One potential risk we face in life is the fear of being judged, ridiculed, or shamed for who we truly are. As young children, we are often open and expressive, willing to be vulnerable and honest. We may not yet understand that others can shame us for showing our authentic selves. While we may have had a strong foundation in terms of physical safety, food, and shelter, we need to consider the safety of our authentic self.

The energy present in the sacral chakra is that of shame, particularly shame around our identity and authenticity. You may have heard the advice to "just be yourself," but it can be challenging when there is fear surrounding it. You may even struggle to know what your authentic self looks like. To survive, you may have built a mask and ar-

INTRODUCTION

Sacral Chakra

mor, creating a false identity that poses fewer risks of being shamed.

The chakra system consists of seven chakras aligned in the center of our body, stacked on top of one another. When fear lives in the root chakra and undermines the very foundation., it inevitably impacts the sacral chakra. Water is the element associated with the sacral chakra, and water moves in an ebb and flow, bending around obstacles and finding ways to continue flowing even through the smallest cracks.

When your foundation is compromised and you don't feel safe, it becomes challenging to go with the flow of life. Trusting and surrendering become difficult because they carry risks. Instead, you may find yourself trying to control every aspect of your life, seeking a false sense of safety and security. The need for control arises to eliminate potential risks, rather than having the confidence to navigate life's obstacles with flexibility and resilience.

Kurt Cobain from Nirvana once said; "I'd rather be hated for who I am, than loved for who I am not." This quote speaks volumes about the importance of authenticity and staying true to ourselves, even if it means facing criticism or rejection. It encourages us to prioritize our own self-acceptance and self-love over seeking validation from others. By embracing our true selves, flaws, and all, we create the opportunity for genuine connections and relationships that honor and appreciate us for who we truly are.

Why do we often prioritize the fear of rejection from others, while neglecting the self-rejection that occurs within us? Why are we so swift to dismiss and compromise our own authenticity in our quest for acceptance from others? It is my sincere hope that we can all strive to embody the essence of this quote and bring about positive change in ourselves and the world around us.

Chakra #3 — Solar Plexus

The third chakra in the chakra system is the Solar Plexus, located above the navel. It governs the stomach, digestive system, rib cage, and nervous system. The element associated with the solar plexus is fire, and its color is yellow. Fire represents a masculine energy, characterized by action, performance, competition, passion, and execution. The solar plexus is linked to personal power, self-esteem, confidence, and boundaries. Personal power is the ability to express our true will and desires without fearing rejection.

If you experience digestive issues, it may indicate a compromised solar plexus. The fear stored in the root chakra can send signals through the nervous system, triggering a response in the brain that perceives potential danger. This disrupts the normal functioning of the digestive system unless the underlying trauma is healed at its root.

Being in a state of survival often leads to adopting a victim mentality, which leaves you feeling powerless in your own life. As young children, we depend on adults to care for us, making us victims of unhealthy or abusive environments. However, as we transition into adulthood, we have a choice: to remain in the energy of victimhood or to reclaim our power by healing the trauma and reintegrating the missing pieces of our soul.

The solar plexus develops during adolescence, between the ages of 13 and 18. This is a phase where we begin to express our personal power and true will. However, trauma

Solar Plexus Chakra

causes our true selves to disappear, along with fragments of our soul. As these soul fragments leave our body and mind, we become weaker and start depending on external sources to compensate for the loss. Allowing others to control us leaves us feeling weak in the solar plexus, stifling the fire within us.

To fill the void and find fulfillment, we unconsciously seek external validation through guilt and manipulation. Guilt energy resides in the solar plexus, which often leads us to operate from this chakra rather than from the heart. Instead of connecting with others from a place of unconditional love and without attachments, we engage through the solar plexus. We feel pulled by others, and we also pull from them through this chakra. Instead of each individual standing in their own power, within their own boundaries, and being fully independent, we rely on one another in an unsustainable exchange of energy. The only truly sustainable, renewable, and divine energy comes from the heart—the life force energy.

Codependency involves seeking external validation and approval from others. In our search to numb the pain and wounds of trauma, we may repress our emotions by turning to food, alcohol, social media, or other external sources, which can become addictions. We look for anything to fill the void within ourselves, longing for a sense of self and wholeness. When our soul is complete, we no longer seek approval, as we know we are enough.

A compromised solar plexus often manifests as procrastination. Procrastination is not laziness but is linked to trauma. It stems from a lack of self-esteem, fear of criticism and judgment, and the fear in the root chakra that blocks us from taking action and following our intuition. When we fear rejection, it becomes challenging to act on our ideas or express our true selves. Our creations lose their purity when we seek validation and compare ourselves to others, choosing conformity over embracing our uniqueness. Additionally, trauma may have fragmented our soul, containing pieces of our authentic self, our True Essence.

Soul Mending is designed to help you retrieve those missing pieces of your soul and reclaim your power. Once you are firmly rooted in your personal power, you can open your heart and experience the world from a place of love, compassion, and abundance, rather than from a place of fear and lack.

Chakra #4 — Heart

The fourth chakra, known as the heart chakra, is located at the center of the chakra system. It serves as a portal connecting us to all living beings, including trees, birds, the sun, the air, and other people. The heart chakra allows us to connect with life force energy, also known as Chi. It governs the lungs, chest, arms, and hands. The element associated with the heart chakra is air, and its color is green. In addition to the main heart chakra, there is an outer heart chakra often referred to as the higher heart chakra, located around the heart chakra. The color associated with the higher heart chakra is pink.

Our heart enables us to connect with everything, including our authentic self and true essence. Our true essence, our light, is unique and holds a special frequency within each of us. However, when we experience trauma, our heart chakra starts to block the connection to our authentic self, causing us to disconnect from parts of our soul.

INTRODUCTION

Heart Chakra

These soul fragments do not disappear but remain within us, residing in the shadows as we have cut them off from the light.

The heart chakra serves as the main portal, a doorway to Source, God, and the entire universe. It is the center of love energy, and through the heart chakra, we can transform the energy of fear into the energy of love. Energy cannot be created or destroyed; it can only change from one form to another. Soul Mending involves taking the fear from the root chakra and filtering it through the heart, allowing for the transmutation of energies. This shift in frequency elevates our entire being, raising us to a higher vibration. It also involves reclaiming the disconnected soul fragments and bringing them home, thereby healing the root of our fears and releasing the fears from the root.

Humans act as filtering systems, much like trees filter carbon dioxide and transmute it into oxygen. Similarly, we can take the fear in our root chakra and filter it through our heart, releasing love into the world. Through this process, we reconnect with our lost soul parts, those precious fragments we have long been disconnected from. By healing ourselves, we contribute to the healing of the world around us.

The heart chakra is our home. Although we may feel that our soul has left our body and mind, we are always connected and always at home. Soul Mending shows us how to reestablish that connection with our soul fragments using our heart chakra.

The development of the heart chakra occurs in early adulthood, typically between the ages of 20 and 29. During this phase, we are ready to form deeper connections with others and the world around us. However, if our heart chakra is closed or blocked due to fear in the root chakra, it becomes challenging to establish meaningful connections. When our heart is closed, it becomes difficult to receive love, create strong bonds, or truly connect with others. The armor and mask we wear to protect ourselves hinder our ability to establish authentic connections.

The heart chakra is associated with love, compassion, joy, and forgiveness. Releasing the fear from our root chakra and using our heart chakra as a filter naturally opens our heart. An open heart anchors us to everything, infusing meaning into our lives and allowing us to surrender and embrace our true authentic selves. It reconnects us to the spirit, as we are born of spirit, leading us back to our true essence.

A healed and open heart liberates us from the codependent energy of the solar plexus, enabling us to embody our true authentic selves. It allows us to view others with compassion and non-judgment, providing opportunities for forgiveness. Through forgiveness, we release attachments to people or events that have caused us harm. This release frees us from being tethered to outdated value systems, unhealthy beliefs, and limited thinking. It teaches us that we are more than what we have been led to believe.

When our heart is open, our light can shine through. Suffering arises from the disconnection with our light, our true authentic selves. As humanity, we are called to heal our traumas and open our heart chakras. A healed heart holds the power to guide us towards making the best decisions and choices, not only for ourselves but also for others and our planet. When we heal the wounds within our hearts, we gain a deeper understanding of compassion, empathy, and interconnectedness.

SOUL MENDING

Suffering arises from the disconnection with our light, our true authentic selves.

A healed heart allows us to see beyond our individual perspectives and embrace a more holistic view of the world. It enables us to recognize the inherent value of every living being and the intricate web of life that sustains us. With a healed heart, we can make choices that promote harmony, respect, and sustainability, both in our personal lives and in our relationship with the Earth.

By fostering love, forgiveness, and healing within our hearts, we contribute to the collective well-being and create a ripple effect of positive change. It is through this transformative process that we can align our actions with our values, making choices that honor the interconnectedness of all life and contribute to the flourishing of our precious planet.

May we strive to heal our hearts, individually and collectively, so that we may walk this Earth with love, wisdom, and reverence, making decisions and choices that serve the highest good of all beings and the beautiful, interconnected tapestry of life.

Chakra #5 — Throat

The throat chakra, also known as the fifth chakra, is situated in the throat area and extends to the top of the shoulders, neck, jaw, teeth, mouth, ears, and nose. Its essence is connected to the element of space, and its characteristic color is blue. The throat chakra signifies a transformative shift into higher frequencies, inviting us to explore the realms beyond our physical reality.

The development and maturation of the throat chakra often occur during the period of our early thirties to mid-forties, typically between the ages of 30 and 44. This phase

Throat Chakra

in life is marked by a readiness to communicate and share our unique voice with the world. However, it is crucial that we express our true essence rather than adopting a voice filtered through fear or societal expectations. The throat chakra is deeply intertwined with truth, communication, and active listening. When this chakra is obstructed or imbalanced, we may find ourselves censoring our thoughts, hesitating to freely express our needs and true will. To authentically express ourselves, we must cultivate a sense of safety and security within.

The solar plexus chakra also plays a significant role in the throat chakra's functioning. When the solar plexus is strong and empowered, we can confidently articulate our true intentions and speak our truth. Our ability to freely express ourselves may be hindered when we are not fully connected to our personal power. Fear in the root chakra, can reverberate throughout the entire energetic system and impede our capacity to speak our truth. It may manifest as a fear of hurting others, a fear of rejection, or a lack of confidence in our own voice.

It is important to differentiate between speaking our mind and speaking our truth. Speaking our mind often arises from a place of fear, powerlessness, and the need to assert ourselves to avoid being taken advantage of. In contrast, speaking our truth emanates from the depths of our heart. The truth is short, it is never followed by an explanation, justification, or elaboration. It stands unwavering and unaffected by external challenges or emotional attachments.

Being mindful of our communication style and how we express our truth is crucial. Do we frequently find ourselves justifying our words? Are we overly concerned about how

The truth is short, it is never followed by an explanation, justification, or elaboration.

others will receive our truth? Do we attempt to manage or control their reactions? It is not our responsibility to manage the emotions of others, just as it is not their responsibility to manage ours. Such dynamics may indicate codependency, emphasizing the direct influence between the solar plexus and throat chakras.

Speaking our truth is not always an easy endeavor, but as we heal and release fear from the root chakra, our truth will naturally flow without force or resistance. A crucial beginning is to observe our communication patterns without judgment. Awareness is the catalyst for healing and transformation. With self-compassion, we can gradually make shifts and adjustments.

The truth holds immense power. When we speak our truth in alignment with the universal truth, we harmonize with our higher selves. As we heal and evolve, we will find ourselves naturally and more frequently speaking our truth, allowing our throat chakra to open and expand. Our voice may undergo a transformation in vibration and frequency, resonating at a profound level. Our words will carry deep significance, reaching and touching others on a soulful level. Speaking from the heart, devoid of powerlessness and fear, will become second nature. We may also discover the art of active listening, valuing the importance of silence and genuinely hearing others. Communication will become smoother and easier as emotions such as fear, shame, and guilt no longer exert influence over our words.

It is important to understand that expressing your truth may lead to changes, and while you may experience the departure of people or things from your life, they are not truly losses. When we are prepared to express our truth, we must also be prepared for the possibility of things shifting and breaking apart. It is through the conflicts and chaos that healing often takes place. We tend to invest a great deal of energy in maintaining peace and preserving things just as they are, but it's important to recognize that meaningful changes cannot occur without some level of disruption. Voicing your truth does not result in losses; instead, it represents a process of realignment.

Chakra #6 – Third Eye

The sixth chakra, known as the third eye, is located on the forehead between the eyes. It encompasses the pineal gland at the lower back of the head and the eyes. The third eye chakra is associated with clairvoyance, intuition, and the ability to perceive the invisible. Its color is indigo, and its element is light. The third eye chakra allows us to see beyond the physical realm.

We typically develop our third eye chakra in our forties, a time when we start seeing the world from a different perspective and in a new light. We begin to perceive life from various angles rather than through a black-and-white lens. It is common to start questioning our existence and wondering if there is more to life than what meets the eye. While these questions may arise at any point in life, they often become more prominent during this period. Curiosity awakens, and we contemplate the possibilities beyond our day-to-day experiences.

A balanced third eye chakra empowers us to rely on our intuition and perception when making decisions. We can see people and situations for what they truly are, not just what they appear to be on the surface. Perhaps you have experienced situations where someone is speaking, and

INTRODUCTION

Third Eye Chakra

you sense that there is more to their words. Some individuals can feel and perceive these subtleties in great detail. The person speaking may not be intentionally deceptive; rather, they are wearing a metaphorical mask, much like many of us do. With a clear and healthy third eye, we can begin to see beyond these masks, both in others and in ourselves.

Many people attempt to forcefully open their third eye because they yearn to see things beyond the physical realm and explore the vastness of the universe. However, this approach is not advisable. Your third eye will naturally open and expand as you engage in the healing process. There are accounts of individuals who have faced significant challenges in returning to a grounded state after a sudden and intense third eye opening. Such experiences can be destabilizing and disorienting.

The key is to focus on healing the fear in the root chakra, and the rest will follow naturally. Forcing the opening of the third eye can create imbalances and unsettle your overall well-being. Allow the process to unfold gradually and at a pace that maintains stability and alignment within yourself.

Chakra #7 — Crown

The seventh chakra, known as the crown chakra, is located at the top of the head and around the forehead area. It is associated with thoughts, awareness, and consciousness. As you engage in the healing process, your crown chakra expands, and your perspective undergoes a shift and expansion. The symbol of the eagle is often associated with the crown chakra, representing the ability to see things from a

INTRODUCTION

Crown Chakra

higher perspective. During your journey of Soul Mending, you will begin to perceive things from a significantly different angle. You will gain multiple perspectives on your traumas, not just from your own limited viewpoint.

The element associated with the crown chakra is the ether. In ancient Greek beliefs, ether was considered a godlike element that facilitated human connection to spirituality and intuition. The colors violet and white are attributed to the crown chakra, representing high frequencies. When we think of these colors, we may associate them with Archangel Michael, the angelic realm, and other spiritual beings in higher dimensions. Many individuals report seeing the color violet during deep meditation, which can signify a connection to higher dimensions and one's higher self. The higher self represents the highest energetic version of oneself.

The root chakra has a significant impact on the entire chakra system, including the crown chakra. When fear is triggered in the root chakra, it sends a signal up the spine and into the brain, affecting the crown chakra and causing confusion. I often encounter clients who have excessive energy stuck in their heads and crown chakras due to overthinking and overanalyzing. This energetic pattern indicates that they are in survival mode, and their minds are desperately trying to keep them safe. It manifests as a cloud-like energy, resulting in a foggy mind. Being excessively caught up in our thoughts is a sign that healing is necessary.

How can clear decisions be made when the mind is overwhelmed? It becomes challenging to envision the long-term consequences, and impulsive decisions are made to navigate immediate survival. Headaches and migraines can also be signs of stagnant energy in the crown chakra. That constant chatter in your mind is caused by fear residing in your root chakra. The inner critic that constantly speaks negatively is a product of the trauma you have experienced. However, once you heal those wounds, the mind becomes quiet. A quiet mind brings freedom and inner peace.

Chapter 2

Fragmentation

How to Identify Fragmentation within You

Soul fragmentation can occur because of trauma when the pain becomes too overwhelming for us to bear. Parts of our soul may leave the mind and body, leading to a sense of dis-ease and not feeling like ourselves.

To determine if you are fragmented, you can ask yourself the following questions:

- *Do I feel scattered and uncentered?*
- *Am I constantly overthinking?*
- *Am I unable to fully focus and concentrate?*
- *Do I feel joy in my life?*
- *Am I searching for my purpose?*
- *Do I feel tired, drained, and uninspired?*

- *Do I regularly feel sad, angry, guilty, ashamed, or afraid?*
- *Am I depressed?*
- *Do I have anxiety?*
- *Do I experience physical pain and discomfort?*
- *Have I experienced a traumatic event in my life?*
- *Did I experience childhood abuse?*
- *Do I feel disconnected?*
- *Do I find it challenging to fully be in the present moment?*

If you answered "yes" to any of these questions, it indicates that you may be experiencing fragmentation. The truth is, we all carry some degree of fragmentation because we have all experienced trauma to some extent.

Your emotions are a clear indicator of fragmentation. Emotions are energies in motion, and they are not meant to remain locked and stagnant within our bodies. They are meant to flow through and out of us. Lower vibrational energies, such as fear, shame, guilt, anger, and sadness, often reside in the lower regions of our bodies, specifically from the chest down. These energies can become stagnant, causing discomfort and a sense of unease within us. However, when we embark on our healing journey and consciously work to release these energies, we create space for a profound transformation to occur. As we let go of these lower vibrational energies, we first open ourselves to the transformative power of neutrality. Neutrality is a state of balance and harmony where higher, more positive energies can flow freely through our being, leading to a renewed sense of well-being and wholeness.

Neutrality is an interesting state to be in because we become less triggered by the external world, and we may mistakenly believe that we simply don't care anymore. But, we have released the heavy emotions that once resided within us. We have healed the wounds in such a way that they are no longer susceptible to triggering. We are finally free!

As we heal, we begin to experience love, joy, peace, and enlightenment. This indicates that we are connecting with higher-frequency energies. These energies flow in and out of our bodies more effortlessly because we have become comfortable with them. They are familiar to our soul. Accessing these high frequencies requires a healed and open heart. If you don't feel love, joy, peace, and enlightenment, it's time to clear your body of the lower vibrational energies that stem from trauma. Soul Mending will guide you in identifying and releasing these fears by following a few simple steps. You will learn to move through your heart chakra and transmute fear into love, reconnecting with your true authentic self.

In our journey of personal growth and self-discovery, it is essential to break free from the habit of categorizing emotions as either positive or negative, good, or bad. Emotions, at their core, are neutral expressions of our inner experiences. They serve as valuable messengers, providing insights and wisdom about our thoughts, feelings, and needs. By letting go of the tendency to judge or label emotions, we open ourselves up to a deeper connection with our inner world.

Instead of fearing certain emotions as harmful or detrimental, we can approach them as energetic experiences that hold valuable lessons. Every emotion carries its unique information and offers an opportunity for self-reflection and growth. By embracing this shift in perspective, we create space to explore the full spectrum of our emotional landscape without resistance or avoidance.

This shift in mindset empowers us to fully embrace our emotions and learn from them. It allows us to delve into the richness of our emotional tapestry, gaining a deeper understanding of ourselves and others. As we cultivate this acceptance, we develop greater authenticity and self-awareness, enabling us to navigate life with resilience and grace.

When we embrace emotions as they are, free from judgment, we grant ourselves the freedom to fully experience and express our true selves. We create a safe and nurturing environment within ourselves, where our emotions are honored and acknowledged. This fosters emotional resilience, enabling us to navigate life's challenges with greater ease and compassion.

By understanding that emotions are natural and valuable aspects of the human experience, we deepen our connection to ourselves and others. We develop empathy and compassion, recognizing that each person's emotional journey is unique and deserving of understanding. This broader perspective not only enriches our own lives but also cultivates harmonious and authentic relationships with those around us.

In this self-help book, we embark on a transformative exploration of emotions, inviting you to embrace the fullness of your emotional landscape. By embracing emotions as they are, you will discover a newfound freedom to express yourself authentically and live a life of emotional resilience, fulfillment, and connection.

Remember, your emotions are your allies on this journey of self-discovery. Embrace them, learn from them, and let them guide you towards a deeper understanding of yourself and the beautiful complexity of the human experience.

Lower energies such as sadness, anger, guilt, shame, and fear may not contribute to our overall well-being, but when we create a supportive space for them and approach them with compassion and love, they can be released from our bodies. Holding space for our emotions means allowing ourselves to fully experience them instead of suppressing or ignoring them. During the Soul Mending process, you will have the opportunity to connect your emotions to specific events or memories, and it is likely that you will feel the emotions associated with those traumas. Simply allow your body to process and release these emotions. Trust in the wisdom of your body to navigate this process. Your mind doesn't need to interfere or seek precise origins or causes for the emotions. Just allow yourself to feel them. It is common to have concerns about getting stuck in an emotion once we connect with it. However, on average, an emotion arises and is felt for about 30 seconds to a minute before naturally dissipating. That's the typical duration of an emotional wave.

In times of discomfort, it is common for us to employ coping mechanisms and seek immediate soothing. However, I invite you to consider an alternative approach. Instead of immediately seeking soothing, allow the emotional trigger to arise within your body. Embrace this moment as an opportunity to delve into your wounds and explore them. Each day, we encounter different situations that offer us opportunities for healing, and it is crucial not to overlook them. Rather than allowing your inner dialogue to take control, let the trigger arise and courageously explore where the underlying wound lies. Remember, you are intimately connected with the world around you, and everything is intricately woven to support you in your healing journey. Embrace these opportunities and seize them with open arms, for they hold immense potential for growth and transformation. Allow yourself to fully experience the pain and discomfort that the trigger is evoking within you, for within that very discomfort lies the potential for healing and growth.

A notable outcome of Soul Mealing is the quieting of the mind. Are you familiar with the continuous stream of thoughts that occupy your mind? Do you find yourself engaged in internal conversations that urge caution or push you to strive for more? Perhaps there is an inner voice that attempts to soothe you during moments of stress. This ceaseless mental chatter is often indicative of a fragmented soul. When trauma triggers the brain's survival mode, it seeks solutions to fears that may not necessarily be rational. However, through the process of healing trauma and releasing fear, the mind can find rest, and the inner dialogue begins to subside. As a result, your mind can reclaim its intended role as a tool—a storage of knowledge—while your heart takes on a more prominent role in guiding your actions and experiences.

Soul Mending is designed to heal trauma at the subconscious level, where it is stored. Many individuals with childhood traumas may have little memory of their early years, and this can be a sign of fragmentation. Memories may seem blurry and out of order. It is fascinating to witness clients during Soul Mending sessions as they access memories they had forgotten, recalling even the smallest details such as their favorite toys, the clothing they wore, and the appearance of their room.

To retrieve fragmented soul parts and integrate them

FRAGMENTATION

Allow yourself to fully experience the pain and discomfort that the trigger is evoking within you, for within that very discomfort lies the potential for healing and growth.

back into your body and mind, you must journey to your subconscious where they are kept. You revisit the moment or event where the fragmentation occurred and provide love and light to that experience, creating a safe space for the fragment to return. We often dismiss or forget about our experiences, putting them aside. However, through Soul Mending, you can uncover how these dismissed events have affected and continue to affect your life.

By addressing the root causes of your thoughts, you can create profound changes in your life. Instead of focusing solely on changing your thoughts, Soul Mending allows you to delve into the origins of those thoughts. Trauma in the root chakra can affect the mind, so it is essential to heal at the root. Soul Mending provides a pathway to healing trauma, integrating fragmented parts of your soul, and reclaiming your true authentic self.

My spirit guides showed me an image of a tree which demonstrates how trauma affects the entire energetic system.

Just like a tree, our being is composed of interconnected energy centers known as chakras, with the root chakra being the foundation of our energetic system. It is here, in the root chakra, that the roots of fear take hold and influence our thoughts, emotions, and physical well-being.

When we experience fear and trauma, these emotions become deeply embedded in the root chakra, affecting our sense of safety, stability, and connection to the world. Just as the tree draws nourishment from its roots, our energetic system absorbs and internalizes the vibrations of fear, which can disrupt the harmonious flow of energy throughout our entire being.

However, through the process of Soul Mending, we be-

FRAGMENTATION

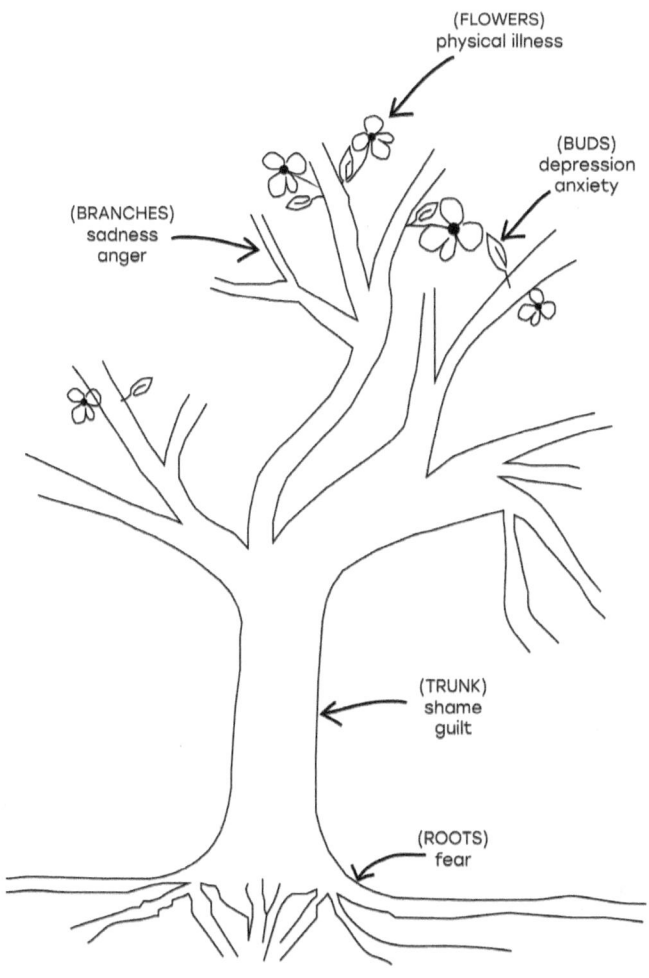

Soul Mending Tree

gin to address and heal the root of fear in the chakra system. Like tending to a garden, we nurture our energetic roots, allowing them to become free from the entanglements of fear and trauma. As we work through this healing journey, we release the grip that fear has held on our body and mind, creating space for growth, resilience, and a renewed sense of inner harmony.

How to Overcome Trauma and Heal from Fragmentation

Overcoming trauma is possible, and the process of healing doesn't have to be long and arduous. Each person's healing journey is unique, and the timeline for healing may vary, but the important thing is that you can heal and transform.

By letting go of the fear associated with trauma and consciously working with your own body and energetic system, you can transmute the energy of fear into the energy of love. This transformation allows you to release the weight of pain and reclaim your true self. Opening your heart chakra and reconnecting with your authentic self are integral parts of this process.

Inviting the fragmented parts of your soul back and integrating them into your body and mind is a powerful aspect of healing from fragmentation. When these fragments return home, you will experience a profound shift within yourself. You will feel whole, present, calm, and empowered. Your perspective on life will change, and you will no longer feel like a victim but an active participant in your own life. This newfound power enables you to make choices aligned with your authentic self.

The effects of Soul Mending extend beyond the emotional and spiritual aspects and can also have physical manifestations. Individuals often become more present in their bodies, leading to a heightened experience of their physical world. When someone has experienced trauma, they may develop a disconnection from their body as a means of self-protection. This disconnection can result in feeling detached or numb, and it can limit the ability to fully engage with and appreciate the physical sensations and experiences of life.

Through the healing process of Soul Mending, individuals can begin to reconnect with their bodies and cultivate a deeper sense of embodiment. This enhanced presence in the body allows them to fully experience the physical world around them. They may notice sensations more acutely, such as the warmth of the sun on their skin, the taste of food, the feeling of movement, or the beauty of nature.

By being more present in their bodies, individuals can also develop a greater sense of self-awareness. They become attuned to their physical needs, emotions, and intuitive signals, which enables them to make choices and take actions that align with their authentic selves. This embodiment and presence in the physical world can bring a profound sense of joy, vitality, and connection to life.

It's important to note that the process of becoming more present in the body and experiencing the physical world more profoundly may vary from person to person. It can be a gradual and ongoing journey of self-discovery and healing. Overall, the healing and integration achieved through Soul Mending can result in a deeper connection to the physical world, allowing individuals to engage with life's experiences in a more profound and meaningful way.

Soul Mending goes beyond the healing of trauma, offering profound benefits that extend to various aspects of your being. As you engage in this transformative process, you will find that it not only addresses the wounds of the past but also deepens your connection to your soul, strengthens your intuition, and fosters self-love and compassion.

Through Soul Mending, you embark on a sacred exploration of your inner landscape, allowing you to establish a deeper connection with your soul. By embracing this journey, you open the door to discovering the wisdom, guidance, and innate gifts that reside within you. As you mend the fragmented parts of your soul, you experience a profound sense of reunion and integration, aligning yourself with your authentic essence.

One of the remarkable outcomes of Soul Mending is the deepening of your intuition. As you heal and release the layers of fear and trauma, you create space for the intuitive voice within you to be heard. Your intuition becomes a trusted guide, offering insights and guidance on your path of self-discovery and healing. This heightened connection to your intuition empowers you to make decisions aligned with your soul's purpose and navigate life with greater clarity and wisdom.

Soul Mending also nurtures self-love and compassion. Through the process, you learn to embrace all aspects of yourself, including the wounded parts that have been fragmented by trauma. As you extend love and compassion to these parts, you create a nurturing environment for healing and transformation. This journey of self-love and compassion allows you to cultivate a deep sense of acceptance and appreciation for yourself, fostering a profound sense of wholeness and inner peace.

It's important to note that Soul Mending is a gentle and

individualized process that respects your unique readiness to heal. The timing of reconnecting with your soul fragments may vary from person to person. Some may experience a swift reconnection, while others may require more time and patience. It is essential to trust in the unfolding of the process, allowing it to naturally guide you towards healing and integration.

Persistence and commitment are vital on the Soul Mending journey. Healing is a transformative and ongoing process that requires dedication and a willingness to face and release the layers of trauma. By staying committed to your healing journey, even during challenging times, you create a space for profound growth and transformation. Embrace the process with patience and trust, knowing that each step forward brings you closer to reclaiming your wholeness and living a life of joy, purpose, and authenticity.

Chapter 3

Meet Your Soul

What Your Soul Consists Of

Understanding how our soul works and what it is made of is crucial for our healing and growth. I have a vivid memory of sitting in my car one day, waiting to pick up my daughter from school, when a sudden and thought-provoking question crossed my mind: What is the true nature of a Soul? I connected to my spirit guides and the answer came in so clearly. Our soul consists of two important parts: Spirit and Ego, representing the Divine Feminine and Divine Masculine energies within us, regardless of gender.

Your Spirit, also referred to as your True Essence, is your authentic self. It is the unique expression of who you are. It can be perceived as the embodiment of the nurturing and intuitive qualities within your soul, often associated with the Divine Feminine. Your Spirit is born from Source or the divine creator and encompasses your creativity, intuition, inspiration, and connectedness to all. It is the energy of being, where you can connect with your higher self and receive guidance. Unfortunately, society has often undervalued and dismissed this aspect of ourselves, prioritizing performance, competition, and adherence to rules rather than embracing our intuition and inner guidance.

On the other hand, your Ego represents your primal drive, your engine for action. It can be viewed as the embodiment of the assertive and logical qualities within your soul, often associated with the Divine Masculine. The Ego's role is to bring your inspirations into tangible form, to execute your ideas and make them accessible to the world. It is responsible for taking action, communicating, and materializing your creative visions. While the Ego is an essential energy for manifestation, it is not sustainable on its own. Relying solely on the Ego can lead to burnout because it is limited in its capacity to create and is primarily focused on execution.

When our Spirit, our true essence, experiences trauma, it can become dimmed and shut down as a survival mechanism. In such instances, we may lean on the Ego, the divine masculine, believing that by performing well, competing, and hiding our true nature, we can be accepted and loved. However, the Ego has often been misunderstood and blamed for being "bad." When we act out of fear, it is our pain talking rather than the Ego itself. The Ego is necessary for our survival and existence, and its purpose is to assist the Spirit in making ideas a reality.

However, when fear takes over, we burden the Ego with additional responsibilities. We ask the Ego to manifest our ideas while causing us the least amount of pain. This leads to playing small, conforming to conventional norms, and comparing ourselves to others to reduce the risk of rejection and humiliation. By imposing these restrictions, we dim our brilliant ideas and prevent them from shining fully in their glory. It's like encountering construction detours and roadblocks on a drive, which frustrate and restrict our progress. These roadblocks and detours represent our fears, which need to be removed and eliminated for us to live freely and allow our ideas to flow and flourish.

The balance between being and doing is essential, just like the balance between the right and left sides of the brain. Your creative ideas and inspirations originate from the right side, while the left side provides organization and analytical abilities. Similarly, your Spirit and Ego are meant to work together harmoniously, supporting, and assisting each other in creating a beautiful reality aligned with your true self.

By understanding the dynamics of our soul and embracing both the Spirit and Ego aspects within us, we can foster a holistic and balanced approach to life. This understanding allows us to heal, grow, and manifest our authentic selves, unencumbered by fears and limitations.

When the Spirit and Ego are not in harmony and synergy, it is often a result of the trauma and pain we carry. Trauma can keep us in survival mode, hindering our ability to trust our intuition and access our divine feminine energy. In such cases, the masculine energy may take over, giving us a false sense of control. Our true essence, our authentic self, becomes fragmented and shattered into many pieces.

Soul Mending offers a beautiful invitation to explore and reconnect with our True Essence, to embrace its beauty and uniqueness. Our soul desires to be fully seen and

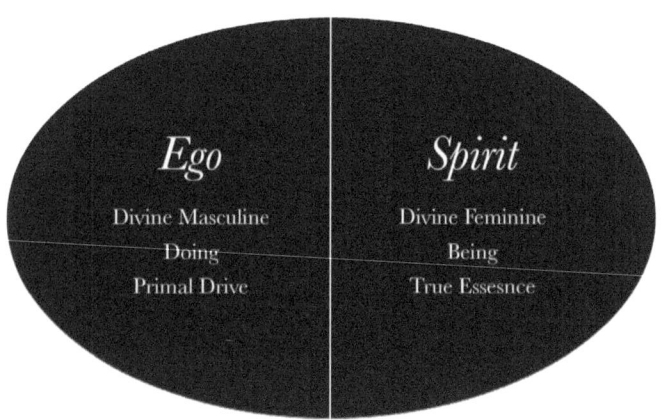

Our Soul

acknowledged. It is ready to undress itself, allowing us to delve deeply into its depths. This journey, though uncomfortable and at times painful, is profoundly rewarding. It is where we can find peace, joy, and freedom. Step by step, we release the strings that hold us back, becoming lighter and shedding the layers that no longer serve us. Through this process, we can simply exist, to let go of expectations and self-imposed limitations.

You are constantly reminded of your inherent limitless nature, transcending the boundaries and limitations imposed by society or any external factors. As you embark on the transformative journey of calling back your fragmented soul parts, you shed the masks and armor that have hindered your true expression. In doing so, you unleash your authentic power and tap into your boundless potential.

The process of reclaiming your soul fragments is a profound act of self-discovery and liberation. It is a journey that allows you to release the shackles of conformity and embrace the full spectrum of who you truly are. As you shed the layers of conditioning and societal expectations, you connect with the depth of your being, recognizing that your essence is vast, expansive, and multifaceted.

Through this journey, you awaken to the truth that you are not meant to be confined or restricted by external standards. You are a unique and extraordinary individual with gifts, talents, and passions that are meant to be expressed freely and authentically. Embracing your expansive nature means embracing your capacity to dream big, think outside the box, and create your own path.

As you shed the limitations that have held you back, you step into a realm of infinite possibilities. You recognize that the power to shape your reality lies within you, and you can transcend any perceived boundaries. Embracing your expansive nature means embracing the truth that you are the author of your own story, capable of rewriting it in a way that aligns with your authentic self.

This journey also invites you to let go of the need for external validation or approval. You realize that your worth and value do not depend on the opinions or judgments of others. Instead, you cultivate a deep sense of self-acceptance and self-love, understanding that your true power emanates from within.

In embracing your expansiveness, you tap into the wellspring of creativity, inspiration, and innovation that resides within you. You are encouraged to follow your passions, explore your interests, and express yourself fully and authentically. Your uniqueness becomes a source of strength and a catalyst for positive change in the world.

As you navigate this journey, remember that it is not a linear process or a destination to be reached. It is an ongoing exploration of self-discovery and self-mastery. Embrace the highs and lows, the twists, and turns, knowing that each experience contributes to your growth and evolution. Trust in your inner guidance and intuition, for they will lead you towards your highest expression and fulfillment.

In the vastness of your being, you are reminded of your infinite potential. Embrace your expansiveness, for you are a powerful force capable of creating a life that reflects your true essence. Break free from the confines of external standards and restrictions, and step boldly into the fullness of who you are. Embrace your limitless nature and allow your light to shine brilliantly, illuminating the path for yourself and inspiring others to do the same.

This very moment offers a significant opportunity to

embark on this transformative journey. Whether you are already on a spiritual healing path and seeking to deepen your healing or just beginning to explore, trust that your soul has led you here for a reason. Follow its guidance and allow it to unfold its wisdom within you.

Fear and Its Effect on Your Soul and Body

Fear often operates unnoticed, like carrying a backpack throughout our lives without realizing its weight until it's removed. We become accustomed to operating from a place of fear, and it becomes our default mode. This fear can take on different forms, such as blocking inspiring ideas, facing constant challenges when chasing our dreams, or even experiencing physical effects like depression and anxiety.

Fear has a profound impact on the choices we make, the decisions we take, the desires we have, and the beliefs we hold. It is common for our perceived wants and needs in life to be influenced by fear, rather than our genuine aspirations. Instead of expressing our true will and embracing the innate desires of our authentic selves, we often make choices and decisions based on fear. These choices serve as a temporary distraction, attempting to mask our pain and wounds. However, each time we prioritize fear over our authentic self's desires, we unknowingly reject our true essence and distance ourselves from our authentic identity.

Fear often originates in childhood when we are vulnerable and deeply connected to our true essence. When we express a facet of our personality and experience ridicule, shame, or judgment, we internalize the pain and develop fear as a protective mechanism. This can lead us to disconnect from our true essence and operate from a survival mode, hypervigilant to avoid pain.

Fear can be all-encompassing, affecting every aspect of our lives and decisions, even the smallest ones. However, by healing and releasing fear, we can create space for love and operate from a heart-centered place. This shift can bring profound changes, allowing us to move through life with love leading the way, experiencing deep connections, and finding joy.

Embarking on a healing journey involves exploring and releasing the emotions and fears connected to our wounds. It requires feeling and acknowledging these emotions, bringing them to the surface and addressing them with love, compassion, and non-judgment. By going deeper and addressing the energetic roots, we can heal and transform in unimaginable ways.

While addressing physical symptoms is important, taking a holistic approach to healing involves looking beyond the surface. Our bodies hold energetic imbalances and disruptions caused by unaddressed emotions and fears. By exploring and understanding the energetic aspects, we gain deeper insights into our healing process.

Fear can create a cascade of reactions and patterns in our lives. For example, the fear of rejection may lead us to build rigid rules and guidelines to protect ourselves, resulting in missed opportunities for deep connections. We adapt to avoid pain, even if it means investing extra time and energy into maintaining these defense mechanisms. However, when we can no longer endure the pain or find new ways to avoid it, we may reach a breaking point, leading to burnout or a realization that deep healing is necessary.

Moving from fear to love requires a deliberate release

of fear energy. This process involves diving deep within ourselves, using our hearts to filter all other energies. Releasing lower vibrational energies creates space for higher vibrational energies, shifting our entire frequency and positively impacting our well-being on multiple levels.

As we release fear and its associated emotions, we move towards neutrality, feeling unaffected and free. We become less triggered by external circumstances and less concerned about others' opinions. This newfound freedom allows us to embrace our authentic selves and connect with our True Essence. We open our hearts even further, embodying the energy of love and its associated qualities, such as acceptance, joy, peace, and, ultimately, enlightenment.

By embarking on this transformative healing journey, we can uncover our true potential, release the limitations imposed by fear, and live a life guided by love, authenticity, and connection.

Chapter 4

Introduction to Soul Mending

A Complete Definition

The concept of Soul Mending is a beautiful and empowering process that focuses on healing and unifying the fragmented aspects of our being. Just as mending a torn piece of clothing brings it back together, Soul Mending aims to mend the separation within ourselves, uniting the fragmented pieces and restoring wholeness.

Soul Mending involves the transmutation of energy, particularly the transformation of fear into love. By engaging the heart chakra, we have the power to change our frequency and vibration, ultimately creating a shift in our reality. Our external world reflects our internal world, and by working on our personal frequency, we can shape our own experiences and create a more aligned and harmonious life.

While Soul Mending can involve receiving support and

holding space from others, it is ultimately a self-healing process. You are your own healer, and the journey of Soul Mending requires you to delve within and explore the depths of your inner world. It is an empowering process that strengthens your intuition and deepens your connection with yourself. You can bring back the fragmented parts of yourself, integrating them into your body and mind, and healing at your own pace.

Soul Mending is for those who are ready and willing to embark on a journey of self-discovery, freeing themselves from the chains of fear and living a life of pain and discontent. It is an invitation to open your heart, reconnect with others, and engage in collective healing. While everyone is responsible for their own healing, it's important to recognize that our personal healing journeys have a profound impact on the people we love and the collective as a whole.

Healing happens in layers, and it's crucial to understand this concept. Like peeling an onion, you remove one layer at a time until you reach the core, indicating complete healing of the wound. You will gradually uncover and heal your wounds, one layer at a time. You don't need to worry about identifying which layer to work on or when, as it happens naturally and organically through the Soul Mending process. Your role is to actively participate in your healing journey by creating a supportive environment and engaging in the process. By doing so, you assist your body in its natural healing process.

By embracing the process of Soul Mending, we can mend the wounds within ourselves, transmute fear into love, and create a more aligned and harmonious existence. It is a transformative path that can bring about profound healing and personal growth.

Chapter 5

Before You Begin

Regulating Your Nervous System

Soul Mending can support the regulation of your nervous system, and you can further aid the process by taking proactive steps to care for yourself physically. By nurturing your body, you can promote a state of relaxation, making it easier to access your subconscious mind during the Soul Mending journey.

Taking care of our physical well-being is an important aspect of any healing journey, including Soul Mending. The nervous system plays a crucial role in our overall well-being and can be deeply affected by trauma, but it is important to recognize that there are additional factors at play as well. Fortunately, there are various ways to achieve this and regulate our nervous system.

1. Establishing a consistent sleep routine and prioritizing restful sleep are essential for the regulation of our nervous system and overall well-being. Sleep plays a crucial role in various aspects of our physical and mental health, including our brain function, emotional well-being, immune system, and overall cognitive performance.

2. Reducing the amount of time we spend using technology and minimizing our exposure to wireless devices can have a positive impact on our nervous system's balance. Constant exposure to screens, electromagnetic fields, and the stimuli of technology can overstimulate our senses and contribute to stress and fatigue.

3. Earthing, also known as grounding, is a practice that involves connecting with the Earth's natural energy by physically touching the ground with bare skin, such as walking barefoot on grass, sand, or soil. This direct contact allows for the transfer of the Earth's electrons into our bodies, which can have a range of potential benefits for our health and well-being.

4. Engaging in activities that involve our hands, such as sewing, pottery, gardening, writing, knitting, or coloring, allows us to be present in the moment and can promote a sense of calmness and focus.

5. Avoiding stimulants such as coffee, chocolate, tea, cigarettes, and alcohol can have a positive impact on promoting a more balanced nervous system. These substances can affect our body's natural equilibrium and potentially contribute to feelings of restlessness, increased heart rate, and heightened stress levels. It's important to note that everyone's tolerance and sensitivity to these substances may vary. Some individuals may be able to toler-

ate moderate amounts without significant effects, while others may be more sensitive and experience stronger reactions.

6. Practicing affirmations and creating a safe space for our emotions can support our emotional well-being and contribute to the healing process. Affirmations are positive statements that we repeat to ourselves to reinforce empowering beliefs and attitudes. When we practice affirmations, we consciously choose words that reflect our desired state of mind and emotions.

7. Reiki and energy healing modalities can be powerful tools for regulating the nervous system and promoting overall well-being. Receiving Reiki energy or exploring other forms of energy healing can help release stagnant energies and restore balance.

8. Meditation is a wonderful practice for calming the body and regulating the nervous system. It's important to approach meditation without expectations or judgment, finding a style and duration that feels comfortable and resonates with you. Setting clear intentions for meditation, whether it's to connect, ground oneself, or receive, can enhance the experience.

9. Our bodies, minds, and souls can also be affected by wireless devices, radio waves, and electromagnetic fields, which can disrupt our natural balance and well-being. Just like a piano or guitar needs tuning to produce harmonious sounds, we also need methods to realign ourselves and restore balance. As mentioned above, earthing can be beneficial, spending time in nature or sound healing is a great way to tune our bodies.

By combining Soul Mending with these practices for regulating the nervous system and supporting the body, we can create a holistic approach to healing and well-being. Each person's journey is unique, so it's important to listen to your body, have patience, and find what works best for you.

Heart Activation Meditation and the Heart Chakra

One powerful practice that can assist in opening and healing the heart chakra is the Heart Activation Meditation. This meditation focuses on bringing awareness and intention to the heart center, allowing it to expand and help release any blockages or stagnant energy. By practicing this meditation regularly, we can create a greater sense of openness, compassion, and love within ourselves.

In addition to practicing Heart Activation Meditation, the symbol TAKA can also be used as a tool to support the opening and healing of the heart chakra. TAKA is a sacred symbol that carries energetic vibrations specifically designed to activate and harmonize the heart center. By incorporating the symbol into our meditation practice or by wearing it as a visual reminder, we can enhance the energetic flow of love, healing, and abundance within our lives.

The heart chakra is a vital energy center located in the middle of the chest, and when it is open and balanced, it can have a profound impact on our overall well-being. An open-heart chakra allows for a greater capacity to give and receive love, experience joy, and cultivate deeper connections with others. It also supports healing on emotional, physical, and spiritual levels.

By engaging in practices like the Heart Activation Meditation and incorporating the TAKA symbol, we can actively work towards opening and healing the heart chakra. Through these practices, we invite more abundance, joy, love, and healing into our lives, creating a greater sense of fulfillment and harmony.

The Heart Activation Meditation, channeled from Archangel Michael, serves to heal the heart, and mend the soul. It is important to approach this meditation with a clear and honest intention. Find a comfortable position, whether lying down or sitting, and create a calm and peaceful environment for yourself. You can choose to play soft meditative music or have silence during the meditation, based on your preference.

If you are practicing the meditation alone, familiarize yourself with the activation meditation beforehand. If someone is guiding you, have them read it slowly and clearly. The duration of the meditation is typically around 10 to 15 minutes, but you can adjust it based on your needs and comfort.

To enhance your experience and direct your attention inward, it is recommended to use an eye mask or scarf, which can create a sense of darkness and help you concentrate on your inner journey. This visual restriction can minimize external distractions and facilitate a deeper and more focused experience during your practice.

During the meditation, allow yourself to relax and be open to the healing energies and intentions of the meditation. Observe any physical sensations, visions, or thoughts that may arise. It is perfectly fine if you don't experience anything specific during the meditation, as each person's experience can vary.

After the meditation, slowly open your eyes and return to your previous state. You may choose to take notes or spend some time in contemplation, reflecting on your experience. Remember that the beauty of this activation meditation is that you can use it at any time to strengthen your connection and keep the channel clear and open.

If you are sharing this activation meditation with someone else or someone is guiding you through it, it can be a profound and supportive experience. Holding space for someone during their activation can create a safe and nurturing environment for their healing process.

You can include this meditation as part of your preparation for the Soul Mending healing journey or as a regular practice throughout the journey. Trust your intuition to decide when it's best to do the meditation. It's a wonderful and adaptable practice that you can use whenever you feel it would be helpful or valuable for your healing process.

Remember to approach this practice with patience, trust, and self-care. Healing and opening the heart chakra is a journey that takes time and varies for everyone. By working on our own healing, we contribute to the collective healing and the well-being of humanity and the planet.

For further guidance and support, you can visit the soulmending.ca website, where you have access to a video of the Heart Activation Meditation and additional resources.

Heart Activation Meditation

"As you stand in the open area surrounded by white light, imagine a path appearing before you. Begin walking along this path, following it until you come across an old stone staircase. Climb the staircase, one step at a time, until you

reach the top.

At the top of the staircase, you see a large ancient wooden door. You notice that it is locked. As you look down, you see a key. Pick up the key and hold it in your hand, feeling its weight and energy. Slowly and deliberately, insert the key into the lock and begin turning it. With each turn, you feel a sense of anticipation and excitement.

As the lock releases, the door swings open wide before you. Beyond the threshold, you see an array of beautiful, multi-colored lights. They shimmer and dance, radiating with vibrant hues of purple, pink, yellow, white, and more. Step through the open door and immerse yourself in this magnificent display of colors and energy.

Feel the warmth and gentle power of the multi-colored lights enveloping you. Allow their energy to wash over you, filling every cell of your being. Absorb their healing and transformative properties, letting them permeate your heart and soul. Bask in the radiance of these lights, knowing that they hold the essence of love, healing, and expansion."

When you are ready to conclude the meditation, express your gratitude for the experience and the healing energies that have been received. Slowly bring your awareness back to the present moment, gently opening your eyes and returning to your surroundings.

After completing the heart activation meditation, take your time to remain in a relaxed state, keeping your eyes closed for an additional 10 to 15 minutes. Allow yourself to fully integrate the energies and experiences from the activation.

During this time, you may continue to feel sensations, visions, or thoughts that arise within you. Embrace them with an open mind and heart, acknowledging their significance in your healing journey. Trust that the activation has initiated a process of awakening and transformation within you, bringing to light aspects of your heart that have long been dormant.

When you feel ready, slowly begin to open your eyes, allowing the transition from the meditative state to the present moment. Take a few moments to ground yourself, feeling the connection between your physical body and the world around you.

Acknowledge the profound shift that has taken place within you, recognizing that the symbol and activation have played a crucial role in unlocking and accessing a deeper part of your heart. Embrace the trust that this process has instilled in you, knowing that you are on a path of healing, growth, and expansion.

It is recommended to journal or reflect upon your experiences and insights following the activation. You may wish to record any thoughts, emotions, or sensations that arose during the meditation, as well as any observations or changes you notice in your life as you continue your soul mending journey.

You can repeat this meditation as often as you like or need, allowing it to deepen your connection with the healing energies and the opening of your heart chakra. Remember, trust in yourself and the process, and honor the transformative power that lies within your heart.

The Taka Symbol

Years ago, I had a strong feeling that I had a book inside me, but I wasn't sure what it would be about. Then, something incredible happened. I started getting messages and visions that revealed a healing process to me. It was like all the pieces of the puzzle came together, showing me a powerful way to help people heal from trauma and overcome their fears. I felt so motivated by this newfound clarity that I decided to start writing.

As I was receiving the information, I was going through the healing process myself. Step by step, I followed the guidance and each time, I felt a little different. I felt my overall health improve. I felt more connected, more joy, and more present. I healed from my traumas and began to see the changes in my relationships, in my work, but more importantly within myself. My healing and the channeling of information was all happening simultaneously, looking back now it was quite a special time in my life.

Every time I sat to write, new information would come in, but at times I would receive information randomly while I was cleaning or cooking. I would stop what I was doing and start writing. I tried to schedule my writing and that didn't always work. So, I let it go and accepted that I wasn't going to control the process of writing just like I didn't control the healing process either. I simply trusted and allowed the information to come to me when the time was right.

The same happened with the Taka symbol. I settled in my healing room where I do my sessions and I sat there. I simply remained open to receive any information at the time. Then it came, a symbol. I couldn't quite see it, but I found myself making gestures with my hands. I started drawing it with my fingers and thought what a strange thing to be doing. I let it go and went on with my day. The following day, I sat there again, and more information came. I saw it clearly drawn in front of me. I wondered where it came from, and Archangel Michael told me that it would soon be revealed to me. A few days later, I found myself sitting quietly again and felt a nudge. I felt like I needed to connect to spirit. I closed my eyes and there it was, this beautiful white energy flowing right in front of me. I didn't understand what it was, until it took shape. There he was, Jesus. He came to me and handed me a book with the word TAKA engraved on it. It was a small brown leather book and as I flipped through the pages, I could see symbols, codes, and words I couldn't understand. He said, it's all there. Any questions I may have, the answers were in there.

The TAKA symbol carries codes and a unique vibration meant to help us heal on a deep cellular level. Trauma is imprinted energetically on a cellular level; therefore, this symbol can help release it. Below is the image of the TAKA symbol. The arrows indicate the direction to draw the lines and the numbers are to indicate the order in which to draw them.

Taka is a symbol of love and compassion and must be used with grace, respect, and integrity. The meaning of the word TAKA is almighty, God the Almighty. You can use the symbol in several ways, you can use it to send energy to people, food, water, plants, pets, etc. There is no limit to what you can do with this symbol—get creative! What is important to remember though is that if you would like to send it to someone, you need their permission. You must let them know that you are sending them energy through you. (Although, the energy would be blocked if it is not meant to be received by the person. Their guides or Archangel Michael would block it.) We must remember that

BEFORE YOU BEGIN

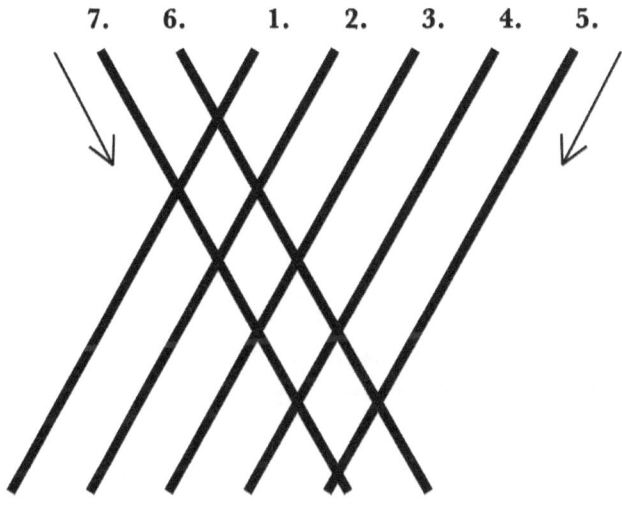

Taka Symbol

even though our intentions are good, sometimes we must not interfere.

There is a specific time where you can use the symbol during the healing process but can be used on its own as well. You can use it for yourself by placing your hands on your heart, but also on any part of your body you intuitively feel like you need. When you are ready to send this energy, draw the symbol in your mind and ask for the energy to flow in through your heart and out from your hands. Then you can place your hands on your plants, food, water, pets, friends, family, etc. Try it from a distance. Ask someone if they are open to receiving this energy and simply imagine them in your mind or have a picture of them and send them the TAKA healing energy. We are energy beings who can connect telepathically with one another. The energies are fluid and expand beyond time and space so it will reach them.

You may be skeptical, but I invite you to keep an open heart and try the Heart Activation Meditation and call on the TAKA symbol. Keep practicing, everything we do gets better with practice. Trust your own process and let go of expectations. Be patient and allow the healing to happen in its own natural course. This is not something you need to rush through, it is a lifetime journey.

Chapter 6

Diving into Soul Mending

An Overview of the Five Steps

The Soul Mending healing process comprises five distinct steps, each serving a unique purpose in the journey of healing and integration. These steps provide structure and guidance, offering a roadmap for your healing journey. However, it is vital to remember that your intuition holds significant importance throughout the process. While reading and keeping the steps in mind, allow your intuition to guide you, granting flexibility and space for your personal healing experience.

Let's begin.

1. *Starting Point*: Selecting a Point of Departure and Exploring Within. Ensuring that your Point of Departure takes the form of a question. A question acts as a com-

pass, providing guidance and direction for your journey.

2. *The Discovery*: Embarking on an Inner Expedition to Uncover and Reestablish a Fragment of the Soul. Discovering the Source of Fear and Exploring its Root Cause.

3. *Going Home*: Reuniting the Fragmented Soul Part with the Self and Finding Wholeness.

4. *Forgiveness*: Healing Through Compassion and Letting Go of Resentment.

5. *Gratitude*: Cultivating Appreciation for Your Inner Light and Journey.

Although this healing process consists of five steps, it can be divided into two distinct parts.

I highly recommend approaching this healing journey in two distinct parts, as it provides a valuable opportunity for integration, assimilation, and deepening the connection with the fragmented parts of your soul. When you embark on the process of reconnecting with these lost aspects of yourself, it is crucial to dedicate ample time to be present with them, to truly understand their emotions, needs, and experiences. This intentional and patient approach allows both you and the fragmented parts to prepare for the eventual reunion, ensuring a harmonious and transformative integration. Keep in mind that you have lived for a considerable period without these soul fragments, and their return may require time and gentle nurturing. While some parts may effortlessly and swiftly reunite with you, signifying that they were long overdue and eagerly awaiting your embrace, others may require more time and attention.

Remember, each part holds its own unique story, wisdom, and healing potential, and by patiently opening the door to their return, you create a space for profound healing, growth, and wholeness to unfold within you.

If you decide to collaborate with a certified Soul Mending practitioner, it is possible to go through all five steps of the healing process within a single session. However, it's important to remember that moving at your own pace is crucial, as faster doesn't necessarily mean better when it comes to healing. Just the act of establishing a connection with a fragmented part of your soul initiates the healing journey. The process of connecting with our fragments holds immense healing power as we finally recognize and illuminate them. This newfound awareness brings forth tremendous healing as we truly see and acknowledge these aspects of ourselves that were once hidden. By shedding light on these fragments, we embark on a transformative path of healing and growth. Remember, the focus should always be on honoring your unique journey and allowing the healing process to unfold in its own time and rhythm.

Part 1: The Initiation (Steps 1 to 3)

During the initiation stage, the emphasis lies in selecting a starting point, exploring within ourselves, and establishing a connection with a fragment of our soul. By nurturing a relationship filled with love and compassion with this part, we can gain valuable wisdom, retrieve lost information, and reintegrate those aspects of ourselves that have been missing. It is vital to invest time in building this connection and allowing for integration and assimilation to occur, as it paves the way for the natural and effective unfolding of the healing process.

Part 2: The Completion (Steps 4 and 5)

The Completion moves into forgiveness and gratitude. Forgiveness can be a challenging but transformative aspect of healing. It involves journeying back to the same place where the fragmented part was discovered and exploring forgiveness towards the person who caused the pain or even towards oneself. This step allows for the release of emotional burdens and the opening of the heart to greater compassion and understanding. Gratitude, on the other hand, invites individuals to acknowledge and appreciate their own light, recognizing their inner strength and growth throughout the healing process.

It's important to note that healing is a personal journey, and everyone will progress at their own pace. The emphasis on patience, self-care, and self-compassion is crucial. There is no right or wrong way to experience this process, and every journey holds valuable lessons and insights.

For those who may struggle with connecting or relaxing during the process, the Heart Activation Meditation can provide support in regulating the nervous system and creating a conducive environment for healing. It's essential to listen to your body's needs and engage in self-care practices to cultivate a state of relaxation and receptivity.

Remember, healing is a lifelong journey, and the inner work you engage in has the potential to bring about profound transformation and growth. Trust in your intuition, be gentle with yourself, and allow the healing to unfold organically. May your Soul Mending journey be filled with healing, self-discovery, and a deepening connection with your authentic self.

The Art of Journeying

Journeying within is a deeply personal and intuitive process of exploring your subconscious space, accessing information, and connecting with different aspects of yourself. Journeying is often performed with the intention of gaining insights, resolving issues, retrieving lost parts of oneself, or seeking guidance from spirit allies or power animals. Indigenous communities have long used journeying to access deeper realms of consciousness that are beyond the reach of the conscious mind.

Traditionally, some indigenous cultures have used hallucinogens as a tool for this purpose. However, today we understand that we can achieve this state without the use of hallucinogens or other substances. There are alternative methods that can induce a theta state of consciousness, such as rhythmic drumming or listening to guided meditations like the Soul Mending Pod on the soulmending.ca website. The guided meditation is designed to relax your psoas muscle and help deactivate your survival instinct, enabling you to enter a more serene state and embark on a journey into your subconscious mind.

It's important to enter a theta state of subconscious awareness where you tap into your intuition as a guide. This involves relinquishing control and embracing your divine feminine energy, which allows you to be in a state of being rather than constantly doing. By accessing this intuitive state of consciousness, you open yourself up to deeper insights and a greater sense of presence.

We are often accustomed to being active and acting, but during the journey, you will be encouraged to relax and simply be. It doesn't require any effort, which can be difficult because we are usually in a constant state of doing. It's important to let go of control and allow our intuition to guide us. Your role is to observe and be present, without the need to actively engage or take charge.

Here are some steps and considerations to help you embark on your inner journey:

1. *Create a Sacred Space*: Find a quiet and comfortable space where you can relax and feel safe. This could be a dedicated healing room, a cozy corner in your home, or anywhere that allows you to focus and feel at ease.

2. *Set an Intention*: Before beginning your journey, set a clear intention or question in your mind. This intention will guide your exploration and provide a sense of direction. It could be related to healing a specific trauma, finding inner guidance, or gaining clarity on a particular aspect of your life. In the Soul Mending process, you want to ask a clear question using a Starting Point, which we will explore later in the book. Remember, A question acts as a compass, providing guidance and direction for your journey.

3. *Relaxation and Grounding*: Take a few moments to relax your body and mind. You can do this through deep breathing, meditation, or any relaxation technique that works for you. Grounding exercises such as visualizing roots extending from your feet into the earth can help you feel centered and connected. Take a moment to shift your focus to your body and become aware of the support it receives from the chair or bed you're sitting or lying on.

4. *Eye Covering and Distraction-Free Environment*: Use an eye mask or cover your eyes with a scarf to create darkness and minimize visual distractions. This allows you to focus inward and enhances your ability to visualize and sense the information that arises during the journey. Ensure that your environment is free from any external noises or disturbances.

5. *Soothing Sounds*: Listening to soothing meditative music or rhythmic drumming can aid in inducing the theta state and accessing the subconscious mind. The type of sounds you choose is a matter of personal preference, if they promote relaxation. Using headphones can be beneficial in eliminating external distractions and enhancing the experience.

6. *Surrender and Trust*: Release any expectations or preconceived notions about what you may encounter during your journey. Surrender to the experience and trust that whatever comes to you is valuable and meaningful. Trust your intuition and the guidance that unfolds within you.

7. *Engage Your Senses*: As you journey, use your senses to interpret the information you receive. Notice any images, feelings, emotions, thoughts, or intuitive knowing that arise. Engage all your senses to fully experience and understand the messages and guidance that come through.

8. *Ask Questions and Explore*: During your journey, you can ask questions to deepen your exploration. Curiosity is key. Ask for clarification, ask for guidance, or simply ask to be shown what you need to see. The more you engage with the information, the more insights and

understanding you can gain.

9. *Practice Regularly*: Journeying is a skill that can be developed with practice. Set aside dedicated time for regular inner journeys to strengthen your intuition, deepen your connection with your subconscious, and receive ongoing healing and guidance.

Journeying can be intimidating for those who are new to it, but I encourage you to persist and not give up. As you continue to practice journeying, you will find that it becomes easier over time. With each journey, you will gain more confidence with the process and become more comfortable with entering an altered state of consciousness.

The more you engage in journeying, the more insights, and experiences you are likely to receive. Journeying opens the door to accessing deeper levels of awareness and connecting with spiritual guidance. It allows you to tap into your intuition and gain valuable wisdom and understanding.

Remember that journeying is a personal and unique experience. Your journeying practice will develop in its own way and at its own pace. Be patient with yourself and trust the process. Each journey holds the potential for growth and discovery, and the more you embrace this practice, the more rewarding it can become.

So, even if it feels challenging at first, keep trying and stay open to the insights and experiences that journeying can bring. With perseverance and an open mind, you will find that the path becomes smoother, and the rewards become greater.

Chapter 7

Step One
Starting Point and Identifying Your Fears

Identifying and understanding your fears is an important step in the healing process. There are three ways to identify your fears within the Soul Mending framework: through emotions, triggers, and physical pain or discomfort. Let's explore each of these starting points further:

1. *Emotions*: Your emotions can provide valuable clues about underlying fears. Take the time to tune in and become aware of your emotional landscape. Notice recurring patterns or intense emotions that arise in certain situations. For example, if you often feel anxious or overwhelmed in social settings, it could be an indicator of a fear of judgment or rejection. Allow yourself to fully experience and explore these emotions without judgment and be curious about what fears may be underlying them.

2. *Triggers*: Triggers are situations, events, or interactions that evoke a strong emotional response or uncomfortable feelings. They can be powerful indicators pointing towards your fears. Pay attention to the specific circumstances or actions that trigger intense reactions within you. Reflect on why these triggers have such a strong impact and what underlying fears they may be connected to.

3. *Physical Pain or Discomfort*: Your body can also provide valuable information about underlying fears. Notice any physical sensations or areas of discomfort that consistently arise in certain situations or contexts. For example, if you experience tightness in your chest or shallow breathing when confronted with a particular challenge, it may be indicative of a fear of vulnerability or being overwhelmed. Pay attention to these physical cues and explore the possible fears connected to them.

As you explore these starting points, it's important to approach the process with curiosity, openness, and self-compassion. Sometimes, the fears we uncover may not be immediately apparent or may differ from what we initially expected. Be willing to dig deeper and question your assumptions. Allow yourself the space to reflect, journal, or seek support from a trusted friend, therapist, or practitioner who can provide guidance and insight.

Remember that healing is a journey, and identifying your fears is a powerful step towards releasing and transforming them. It may take time, patience, and self-reflection, but as you gain awareness and understanding of your fears, you can begin to cultivate self-compassion, develop new perspectives, and take steps towards healing and growth.

Identifying Your Fears through Emotions

Observing and identifying your emotions is an important aspect of this journey. By acknowledging and expressing your emotions, you can gain insight into your fears and underlying beliefs.

Remember that you are not your emotions; you are experiencing them. Using statements like "I feel sad" or "I feel angry" helps create that distinction. Take some time to reflect on the emotions you are currently feeling or often experience. It could be sadness, anger, depression, disconnection, feeling lost, shame, or any other emotions that resonate with you.

Starting where you are emotionally is crucial. There's no need to force anything or search for the perfect starting point. Trust that no matter where you begin, it will most likely lead you to the same destination. Everything is interconnected, and your higher self knows the way. Surrendering to your emotions and accepting them as they are an essential step. Avoid projecting into the future or pressuring yourself to "get over it." Instead, meet yourself where you are emotionally and practice acceptance without judgment.

To begin your Soul Mending journey and connect with a soul fragment, create a comfortable and distraction-free environment. Cover your eyes with an eye covering, such as an eye mask or a scarf, to eliminate visual distractions. You can also listen to soothing music using headphones.

This sets the stage for the journey into your subconscious.

Take a few deep breaths and feel the support of the chair or bed beneath you. Ask for the energy of the highest white light to pour down and create a protective and healing container, known as the Soul Mending Pod. You can find this resource on the soulmending.ca website. The Pod provides a safe space for you to access your subconscious and receive support during the journey.

Once you're ready, focus on the specific emotion you want to explore and ask the question, "What is this emotion trying to tell me?" Asking a question gives your journey direction and purpose.

Allow yourself to travel into your subconscious without trying to control the process with your mind. Your soul and intuition have the answers you seek. Trust whatever way the journey unfolds for you. It might feel like going down a tunnel, and it's essential to go as far as you can and stay as long as you can. At some point, a memory from your past will emerge. If it becomes challenging to sit with the energy, you can come back up, open your eyes, take a deep breath, and try again later. There's no rush, and there's no judgment in this process.

When a memory arises, stay with it and observe it closely. Engage your senses and feel the memory in your body. Notice the surroundings, the people present, the time of day, and any other details that stand out. If you're able to connect with a specific memory, write it down. If not, that's okay too. You can try again when you feel ready.

If you've visited multiple memories in one sitting, choose one to work with. Each time you revisit the process, some memories may re-emerge while others may have already been healed. The healing journey is not linear, and

STEP ONE: STARTING POINT

you can access and heal different parts of yourself at any time.

As you explore your memory or event, consider the presence of others and their words or actions toward you. Pay close attention to your reaction—both physical and emotional. This is the crucial point where you can observe your thoughts and identify the promise you made to yourself in that moment. This promise might involve keeping a part of yourself hidden to avoid experiencing pain again. Recognize that it is at this moment that the seed of fear was planted within you.

By delving into these memories, observing your reactions, and feeling the emotions, you can begin to understand the root of your fears and beliefs. This process allows you to heal and integrate fragmented parts of yourself, bringing you closer to wholeness and self-discovery.

Sometimes, during the healing process, you may not recall a specific memory in a visual form, but instead experience a sense of knowing or understanding. Some individuals have shared that they didn't see the memory visually but had a deep intuition or inner knowing about what it entailed. Others may have encountered objects or words that, through further exploration and questioning, led them to uncover the memory they were seeking. Each person's experience is unique, and the process of recollection can vary from individual to individual.

As you continue your healing journey, you will gain a deeper understanding of how the process works for you personally. It's important to trust in your own unique process and allow your intuition to guide you. Everyone's experience may differ, so it's crucial not to disregard any information that comes to you. Be open and receptive to the insights, messages, and sensations that arise during your journey, as they may hold valuable wisdom and guidance for your healing and growth. Embrace the unfolding of your own intuitive wisdom and honor the knowledge that emerges within you.

Identifying Your Fears through Triggers

Triggers are powerful indicators that something within us needs healing. They can be physical, emotional, or mental responses to external stimuli such as words, actions, events, environments, smells, locations, or sounds. When we are triggered, it immediately touches upon a pain point, offering us an opportunity to delve deeper into our inner selves.

Triggers are blessings in disguise because they provide a clear pathway to the root of our fears. They elicit an instantaneous reaction, both physically and emotionally, highlighting areas within us that require healing. By recognizing and acknowledging these triggers, we can embark on an exploration of the pain points they uncover.

It's crucial not to miss these opportunities for healing. Each time we are triggered, it signifies a fragment of our soul that is seeking healing and release. Triggers help us shed our armor and masks, allowing us to free ourselves from fear. Instead of deflecting or lashing out at others when triggered, it's important to take responsibility for our own healing and introspection.

Being triggered indicates a misalignment within ourselves. If we were anchored and centered in our energy, external circumstances would not easily sway or disturb us. Therefore, it's essential to pause and reflect on the reasons

STEP ONE: STARTING POINT

behind our triggers, rather than blaming others for our reactions. This requires going within, exploring our own inner landscape, and getting curious about the root causes of our discomfort.

When a trigger occurs, whether in the moment or later, we can create a sacred space for ourselves by lying down, covering our eyes, and inviting the white light to surround and accompany us on our journey. By asking a clear and precise question such as "Why did this trigger me?", we open ourselves to receiving insights and messages. Memories or revelations may emerge, shedding light on the deeper wounds and fears we carry.

Although we may not initially appreciate those who trigger us, it's important to recognize that they are catalysts for our healing. By shifting our perspective and seeing triggers as gifts, we can take responsibility for our own growth and embrace the opportunity they provide. Life is working with us, not against us, and when we shift our thinking, we begin to see how everything supports our healing and evolution.

Over time, as we engage in healing work, we may find that we are triggered less frequently. This indicates that we have become more anchored and aligned within ourselves. External circumstances, such as news, comments, or opinions, no longer easily sway us. It signifies a healing process where we release anger, sadness, guilt, shame, and fear from our being. This newfound freedom from triggers allows us to attract new people and opportunities into our lives, as our energy shifts and aligns with a higher vibration.

Whether you're experiencing emotions, triggers, or physical pain, it's important to recognize that healing oc-

SOUL MENDING

*Feel your way through it, not
think your way through it.*

curs through feeling, not just through thinking. Feel your way through it, not think your way through it. You cannot solely rely on your thoughts to navigate the healing process, but rather, you must tap into the power of your emotions and allow yourself to fully feel and process them. By embracing your feelings and giving them space, you create an opportunity for healing to unfold. It is through this process of deeply feeling and acknowledging your emotions that true transformation and healing can take place. Trust the wisdom of your emotions and allow them to guide you on your journey toward wholeness.

It's important to emphasize once again the significance of trusting the information you receive during your journey. Avoid judging or dismissing the information as irrelevant, but instead, embrace it and have faith in its value. Every piece of insight, message, or sensation that comes to you holds significance in your healing process. Trusting the information means allowing it to guide and inform your journey, even if it may not immediately make sense or align with your expectations. Embracing and trusting the information will help you uncover deeper layers of understanding and facilitate your personal growth and healing.

Identifying Your Fears through Physical Pain or Discomfort

The third starting point for healing and self-exploration involves physical pain or discomfort. This can include any form of physical pain, such as soreness, stiffness, or even more severe conditions or illnesses. By connecting with the pain and asking the question, "What is this pain trying to tell me?" we can delve into its underlying message and uncover valuable information.

When working with physical pain, it's important to create a calm and comfortable environment. You can place your hand directly on the area of pain or simply sit or lie down and connect with it. By feeling the pain and allowing it to be present, you open the space for insights and memories to emerge from your subconscious.

Reconnecting with your body and trusting its signals may take time, especially if you have lost touch with it. If you encounter resistance during this process, understand that it serves a purpose. Resistance can be a protective mechanism, preventing you from facing traumas or experiences that you may not be fully ready to confront. It is essential to honor and work with your resistance, allowing it to guide you gently through the healing process. Over time, as healing progresses and energies shift, the resistance may naturally diminish.

Resistance itself can be a starting point for exploration. By asking questions like "Why am I resisting?" or "What am I resisting?" you can uncover deeper layers of understanding and work through the resistance that may be holding you back.

During this healing journey, every piece of information that arises is valuable. Even if you don't receive any immediate insights, that in itself is significant. Everything has a message and meaning, and you are the one best suited to interpret and understand those messages. It can also be helpful to share your experiences and interpretations with someone you trust, who can offer a non-judgmental perspective and support your healing journey.

Once you receive information or insights, take time to sit with them and allow them to unfold. Each layer holds a message, and by unpacking it slowly and letting the energy of the message vibrate through you, you can fully embrace its transformative power. Trust that whatever memories or events come up for healing are connected and intertwined and addressing one can have a ripple effect on others. Often, we see patterns in our lives—similar partners, jobs, friendships—and these patterns are opportunities for healing, although we may initially perceive ourselves as victims.

Throughout this process, you may release and transform different energies in a natural and organic way. It is common to first address sadness and anger, followed by shame and guilt. This progression is designed to gradually build your spiritual strength and readiness to heal deeper aspects of yourself.

With continued practice, journeying within and exploring your energy will become instinctive. You will develop trust in yourself, your higher self, and your spiritual team. Remember that we all have the innate ability to read and heal energy. By following these simple steps, you can tap into your own power of transformation and transmutation.

If you find it challenging to identify a starting point, you can ask questions like "What do I need to heal at this time?" or "What fragment of my soul is ready to come home?" Trust the process and allow the answers to unfold. It's important to give yourself permission to feel the emotions that arise, even if they may be uncomfortable or conflicting. Judging or denying certain emotions only hinders your healing journey. Explore why certain emotions are difficult to allow and inquire further to gain understanding and clarity.

By embracing the process, asking questions, and staying open to the answers that emerge, you can embark on a transformative healing journey that leads to self-discovery, release, and greater alignment with your true self.

It's important to keep in mind that the healing process is not linear, and it can become a bit messy at times. Healing a wound is similar to untangling a ball of yarn, where you need to patiently unravel the knots. This unraveling occurs through curiosity, exploration, and a generous amount of patience. Embrace your healing journey with an open mind and a willingness to delve into the depths of your experiences, trusting that each step you take brings you closer to healing and growth.

While it may seem too simple to just ask a question and expect to uncover a deep emotional wound, the truth is that it can be that straightforward and uncomplicated. If you find yourself unable to access a particular memory, it is likely due to resistance. Your body and mind may be hesitant to approach the pain, so it's important to remind yourself that you are in a safe and supportive environment. By creating a sense of safety, you can help your body and mind overcome resistance and delve into the healing process more effectively.

I cannot emphasize this enough. When you ask the question, trust the answers that arise within you. Avoid dismissing them. Instead, cultivate curiosity and delve deeper into what surfaces. This is the key to unraveling the complexities of your emotional wound, gradually peeling away the layers that have accumulated over time.

Many clients have shared that during the process, they didn't recall a specific memory or receive clear information. Instead, they experienced what seemed like random thoughts. However, as they explored these thoughts further,

STEP ONE: STARTING POINT

*Healing a wound is similar to
untangling a ball of yarn, where you
need to patiently unravel the knots.*

they discovered that these seemingly unrelated thoughts held the answers to their questions. By taking the time to delve deeper into these thoughts and understand their significance, clients soon realized the valuable insights and revelations hidden within them.

A standard Soul Mending journey typically lasts for 30 minutes, so it is important to allocate enough time for your journeying and avoid rushing through the process. These journeys hold a sacred nature and should be approached with reverence, respect, and honor.

Chapter 8

Step Two
The Discovery: Love and Making Contact

Approaching fear with love is a powerful and transformative approach. Love, being a high vibrational energy, has the capacity to transmute fear and bring healing to our inner selves. The heart chakra, which holds the energy of love, becomes a channel through which fear can be alchemized into love, just like turning metal into gold.

In the Soul Mending process, once you have identified a memory from your journey, your present self enters the presence of your past self. This past self could be from any timeframe, and it's important to trust that the revealed memory is what needs healing at this time. As you connect with your past self, approach them slowly and create a safe and trusting space for them. This process may take time, as your past self may be in pain, lacking trust, and fearing further hurt or rejection. Allow your intuition to guide you during this interaction, as it transcends the limitations of the conscious mind and taps into the subconscious.

During this journey, you may be pleasantly surprised by the kindness, love, and compassion your soul exhibits towards your fragmented self. Our conscious mind, often influenced by fear, can be judgmental and resistant. However, when we connect to our intuition and open our hearts, we tap into our authentic, loving selves. Many individuals have shared their amazement at how effortlessly they knew what to say or do, often feeling guided by their intuition. Some have even called upon angels or departed loved ones for assistance, finding wisdom and support from these higher realms. This serves as a reminder that our conscious self is limited, while our soul holds infinite love and understanding.

When you connect with your past self, you may find that they are hesitant to engage with you. They might sit in a corner or turn their back to you. It's important not to force anything during this process. The mere fact that you have been able to connect with this fragmented aspect of yourself is already significant progress. Stay present with your past self, observing their emotions, age, and any other details that come into focus.

As you spend time with your past self, you might engage in activities such as playing, talking, or simply holding each other. This interaction begins to restore a sense of joy and love within. Parenting oneself involves providing comfort and reassurance to the inner child, addressing the root chakra's need for safety and security. By creating a sense of safety, you invite the inner child to feel safe within your own being, to come home.

It's important to note that when journeying back to a painful memory, you are not changing the event itself. Instead, you are changing its impact on you. Events that cause pain and fear leave a dark imprint on your energy field, and through connecting with your fragmented self and offering love and compassion, you transform these lower energies into light. Love is indeed a powerful energy.

During the Soul Mending process, you become an energy reader, attuning to your body and listening to its messages. Your body serves as a sensory tool, communicating with you in its own language. By connecting with your body and reading its energy, you may revisit certain events or memories. Take your time to observe the details, but also trust that if a connection is not made immediately, it means you are not yet ready. The healing process unfolds at its own pace, and when the time is right, you will revisit the memory with greater ease and clarity.

Establishing eye contact with your inner child or past self is a significant and meaningful step in cultivating a genuine connection. Eye contact symbolizes seeing and acknowledging each other, creating a powerful energy exchange. However, it is crucial to trust your intuition throughout this process. If you don't physically experience eye contact but sense a deep connection has been established, honor that intuitive knowing. These steps and guidelines serve as a framework, but it is your intuition that holds the utmost importance in this journey of self-discovery and healing.

Although the explanation may seem extensive, the actual process of establishing a connection with your inner child or past self can occur in just a few minutes for some individuals. Many people have shared transformative experiences where their younger self approached them with open arms, eagerly welcoming their reunion. The connection can be made swiftly and effortlessly, enveloping you in a profound sense of love and acceptance.

When we disconnect from fragmented parts of our soul, we inadvertently lose access to the unique and beautiful aspects that define who we are. These fragmented parts often reside within our inner child, holding the essence of our authenticity and individuality. By consciously reconnecting with our inner child, we embark on a journey of self-discovery and self-acceptance, allowing us to reclaim those inherent traits that make us who we are.

Reconnecting with our inner child involves acknowledging and embracing the qualities, talents, and joys that may have been overshadowed or suppressed over time. It is a process of rediscovering the playfulness, creativity, curiosity, and innocence that are inherent in childhood. As we open ourselves up to this connection, we begin to access the reservoir of unique qualities that lie within us, waiting to be expressed.

By embracing our inner child, we allow ourselves to fully express our true and authentic selves. We tap into the wellspring of authenticity that resides within, giving ourselves permission to be vulnerable, spontaneous, and free from self-imposed limitations. The reintegration of our inner child brings forth a renewed sense of enthusiasm, passion, and zest for life.

As we embrace and honor our inner child, we begin to infuse our daily experiences with a childlike wonder and joy. We approach challenges with resilience, creativity, and a fresh perspective. Our relationships deepen as we connect with others authentically, nurturing a sense of playfulness, empathy, and compassion.

Reconnecting with our inner child is an act of self-love and self-acceptance. It allows us to heal the wounds of the past and cultivate a nurturing and supportive relationship with ourselves. As we engage with our inner child, we extend love, understanding, and forgiveness, fostering a sense of wholeness and integration within.

STEP TWO: THE DISCOVERY

In the process of reconnecting with our inner child, we also gain a deeper understanding of the experiences and events that may have led to fragmentation. We gain insight into the patterns, beliefs, and behaviors that were formed as coping mechanisms in response to past traumas. By addressing these patterns with compassion and understanding, we can release their hold on us and create new pathways for growth and transformation.

Ultimately, embracing our inner child is a transformative and empowering journey. It is an invitation to reclaim our authenticity, to express ourselves fully, and to live a life aligned with our true essence. By nurturing the connection with our inner child, we open ourselves to the infinite possibilities of self-discovery, healing, and personal growth.

It is crucial to approach the Soul Mending process with an open mind, as clients have shared remarkable stories of connecting with their inner child in the most unexpected of places. Each journey is unique and holds its own surprises.

One client, for instance, shared an extraordinary experience of discovering her 4-year-old fragment within the depths of a dark cave. In this unexpected setting, she was able to reconnect with the innocence and vulnerability of her younger self, offering healing and support.

Similarly, another client stumbled upon their 7-year-old fragment in an old apartment they had long forgotten about. As they stepped into this familiar yet distant space, memories flooded back, and they were able to address the pain and wounds that had been carried for so long.

In yet another poignant instance, a client found their 13-year-old self still lingering in the corner of a hospital room. The revelation struck them profoundly, as they realized that the operation they had undergone at that young age had left an unexpected and unhealed emotional trauma.

These encounters with the inner child demonstrate the power of Soul Mending to uncover hidden fragments and address unresolved issues from the past. By revisiting these forgotten or neglected parts of themselves, clients have been able to offer compassion, understanding, and the healing they desperately needed.

These unexpected discoveries serve as powerful reminders that our inner child may reside in places we least expect. It underscores the importance of exploring and embracing the entirety of our personal history to unlock the potential for profound healing and transformation. By keeping an open mind and allowing intuition to guide us, we can embark on a journey of self-discovery and mending that transcends the boundaries of time and place.

The next step in the Soul Mending process is to bring the inner child home, recognizing that home is where the heart resides. This step is crucial for building a strong and nurturing connection before moving forward on the transformative journey towards wholeness and integration.

Bringing the inner child home involves creating a safe and loving space within ourselves where our inner child feels welcomed, accepted, and protected. It is about creating an inner sanctuary where our inner child can freely express themselves, heal, and grow.

To bring the inner child home, we must cultivate an environment of unconditional love, compassion, and understanding. We extend a loving hand and an open heart to our inner child, assuring them that they are safe, valued, and supported. This process requires patience, gentleness, and a willingness to listen to the needs and desires of our inner child.

One powerful way to create a sense of home for our

inner child is through inner dialogue and self-reflection. We engage in compassionate conversations with our inner child, actively listening to their fears, desires, and emotions. We offer reassurance, guidance, and encouragement, just as we would to a beloved child. Through this dialogue, we develop a deeper understanding of our inner child's experiences and needs, forging a stronger connection and sense of trust.

Creating physical and symbolic representations of home can also support the process of bringing the inner child home. We may create a personal sanctuary or sacred space where we can retreat and reconnect with our inner child. This space can be adorned with objects, images, or symbols that evoke a sense of safety, comfort, and joy for our inner child.

Additionally, engaging in activities that bring us joy and nourish our inner child's spirit can be a powerful way to create a homecoming experience. We may explore creative pursuits, play, engage in nature, or participate in activities that spark our inner child's curiosity and sense of wonder. These experiences allow our inner child to feel seen, heard, and valued, fostering a deeper connection and sense of belonging.

Bringing the inner child home sets the foundation for the journey towards wholeness and integration. It establishes a solid relationship with our inner child, creating a container of love and support that will accompany us on our healing path. By embracing and integrating our inner child, we tap into their wisdom, innocence, and joy, infusing our lives with authenticity and vitality.

As we continue our Soul Mending journey, the connection with our inner child serves as a guiding light, reminding us of our true essence and providing insight into our healing and growth. Together with our inner child, we embark on a transformative process of reclaiming our power, releasing old wounds, and embracing the fullness of our being.

By bringing the inner child home, we embark on a profound and transformative journey towards wholeness, authenticity, and integration. It is a journey of self-love, self-discovery, and healing, where the inner child becomes an ally and a source of inner wisdom. Through this process, we create a home within ourselves, a sanctuary where our heart and soul can thrive, and where the transformative power of Soul Mending can unfold.

Chapter 9

Step Three
Going Home

Your heart is the place where your true essence resides. This entire process revolves around identifying fragmented parts of your soul resulting from trauma and reclaiming them by establishing a connection and bringing them back to your core. The ultimate goal is to restore your sense of wholeness and inner peace, dispelling any feelings of fragmentation. The terminology used to describe this process is not as crucial as the actual steps involved. By faithfully following these steps, you will gradually rediscover joy and tranquility in your life.

Now that you have successfully identified a memory and established contact with your younger self, it is time to embark on the journey back home. While all the steps are important, this particular one marks the initiation of an energetic transformation. The healing process commenced when you shed light on the memory associated with the trauma, and now you have the opportunity to transmute that energy. It is time to elevate the vibration of those lower energies and enhance the life force energy within yourself, bringing you closer to alignment.

When you connect with your inner child or past self, reassure them that it is now safe to return home, that they can come back with you. Affirm that the world is a secure place and that their presence is necessary at home. Emphasize that it is emotionally and physically safe for them to exist in this world. You are sincerely requesting that part of yourself to return home. When your inner child is truly ready, a bright portal of light will show up. This radiant portal represents your heart chakra, the gateway through which they will fully integrate with you. The heart chakra will open up and make space for this fragment, simultaneously healing your heart chakra and amplifying the energy of love within your being. It is natural to have concerns about whether the portal will show itself or if you will be able to perceive it, but trust that it will reveal itself at the opportune moment.

Some individuals perceive a brilliant light taking over, confirming the retrieval of their fragmented soul part. Others envision a door that, once opened, fills the room with luminosity. The manifestation of the radiant light can differ, so allow room for your own unique experience. Some individuals have even witnessed its appearance before they explicitly asked their inner child if they were ready to return home. The energies are aware! Visualize it as a large spherical light eagerly awaiting your entrance.

As you take your past self by the hand and prepare to return home, envision the radiant light ahead. It may manifest as a circular glow, resembling a portal you can walk through. This represents your heart opening and inviting your fragmented part to return. Begin walking towards it, gradually passing through the light portal. By doing so, you reintegrate your lost soul fragment into your heart, your body, and your mind. At this point, place your hands on your heart chakra and utter the word "TAKA."

Invoke the TAKA symbol, which will assist in the healing and mending of the fragment within your heart. Keep your hands on your heart chakra for 5 to 10 minutes. This step is crucial to ensure that your soul part has returned and is now safely home. The TAKA symbol works to repair and heal the returned fragmented part, integrating it back into your present self. It serves as a balm for the soul, fostering its mending and restoration.

Once you have completed this step, you may begin to perceive a shift occurring within you. The most common sensation is a pressure on the chest, which may arise shortly after your journey or within a few days. Your heart is gradually healing and opening. Although it might be uncomfortable, remain still and allow the energies to work their magic. Allow the energies to expand.

Your soul is evolving, and growth often entails some discomfort. Grant yourself permission to rest. Avoid rushing your healing journey. Take your time and cultivate patience. If you attempt to heal everything at once and progress too hastily, you risk bypassing the healing process and generating further confusion and inner conflict. The energies have shifted, necessitating a realignment. Your body, mind, and soul need to harmonize and come into alignment. Life is a beautiful dance between you and Spirit. Engage in your personal work, and then allow Spirit to do its work. Utilize your intuition to discern when and what the next step should be. Always remember that you are guided and protected.

It's essential to recognize that each person's healing

journey is deeply personal and unique to their individual experiences. Here, I would like to share a couple of examples of client journeys, illustrating how unique each experience can be.

Client #1: I recall a client who initially held doubts and believed they couldn't establish a connection due to their overthinking nature. However, to their surprise, the process of connection unfolded swiftly, leading them to a profoundly beautiful and healing experience. It all began with a simple yet profound question: "What needs healing at this time?"

As they delved into their inner world, they found themselves transported back to a specific moment when they were just nine years old. In this memory, their younger self lay on the bed, consumed by sadness and fear. The client instantly recognized the trauma, fully aware of what had just transpired in that room. They could feel the weight of the energy and were moved to tears. Yet, something extraordinary occurred—their intuition kicked in, guiding them to lay down beside their inner child.

In that sacred space of vulnerability and compassion, the client expressed deep remorse for the pain and suffering their younger self had endured. They reassured the little child that they were no longer alone and that from this moment forward, they would be there for her. The connection between the client's present self and their inner child grew stronger, and a profound sense of readiness emanated from the young 9-year-old.

Together, hand in hand, they rose from the bed and approached the bedroom door. As they opened it, a radiant light called them forward. Stepping across the threshold, the client knew without a doubt that their fragmented part, the once-lost 9-year-old girl, had finally found her way home. The healing journey had brought them together, reuniting the client with their inner child in a profound moment of transformation and wholeness.

Client #2: This client embarked on a similar journey with a question that resonated deeply within them: "Which fragment of my soul is ready to come home?" As they began their soul mending process, they found themselves standing within a circle, surrounded by numerous fragments of themselves representing different ages and aspects. Most of the fragments seemed eager and happy to see them, except for one fragment. This fragment stood across from them in the circle, facing away and unwilling to make eye contact. Recognizing the importance of patience and honoring the process, the client chose not to rush or force the fragment's participation. Instead, they chose to connect with the other fragments, holding their hands and emanating love towards all of them.

In following journeys, the client revisited the same scene, seeking further connection and understanding. Each time, they approached the resistant fragment with empathy and compassion, knowing intuitively that it needed more time to feel safe and willing to join the circle. The client continued to send love and acceptance to all the fragments, allowing for the gradual healing and integration process to unfold organically. Finally, on a new day, during their third visit, the resistant fragment made the decision to join the circle. As this pivotal moment unfolded, a radiant light appeared, signifying the culmination of the soul mending session. The client vividly expressed the intensity of the pressure they felt in their heart, as it began to open wide, welcoming all the fragments back home.

This profound and transformative soul mending session serves as a powerful reminder of the necessity for patience and gentle persistence in the healing process. It illustrates how healing fragments of the soul requires an understanding of their individual needs and the willingness to create a safe and loving space for their integration. The client's journey demonstrates the beauty and potency of embracing the journey with compassion, trust, and an unwavering commitment to one's own healing and wholeness.

If you have successfully reunited with a fragmented soul part, there are additional steps you can take to support its integration. It has found its home, a place of safety, and it is crucial to provide it with proper care. Recognize its presence. Connect with it. Inquire about its desires and needs. Ensure that you create a compassionate and loving environment, assuring your fragmented part that it will remain with you indefinitely.

Once the soul part, your inner child, has returned, you may experience their emotions more intensely. You might suddenly feel profound sadness or anger. These emotions indicate the child's healing process. It signifies the release of old stagnant energies that were harbored within you. These energies are being liberated and ultimately transformed into higher vibrational energy. Allow this process to unfold. Refrain from involving your mind excessively. Simply be present and receptive to the healing experience.

If you were unable to trace your emotion to a specific memory or event, that is perfectly okay. You can revisit it when you feel ready. Some fears are deeply rooted and require time to unravel and heal. There should be no judgment regarding the speed or effectiveness of your healing journey. It is a gradual process that necessitates openness and acceptance.

STEP THREE: GOING HOME

Seeing the Light

It is understandable that some individuals may feel skeptical about perceiving the portal of light. However, it is important to trust in the process and have faith that it will manifest when the time is right. The appearance of the portal is intricately connected to the readiness of your soul part to return home. The radiant light you witness signifies the opening of your heart, symbolizing its receptivity to the return of your fragmented aspect. This light is imbued with the transformative power of love, acting as a catalyst to transmute fear into love. Remember that energy cannot be destroyed; it can only be transformed or transmuted. In this process, you are actively changing lower vibrational energy into a higher frequency energy. This profound shift will permeate your entire being, both internally and externally. As you alter your inner world, the external world will naturally follow suit. Embrace the transformative power of love and trust in the unfolding of your journey.

Rest

After completing the previous steps, it is advisable to take a rest and allow your inner child, your fragmented soul part, time to integrate. This period of integration is crucial for the healing process. It is common to experience intense emotions in the days following this journey. Take this time to nurture yourself and create a safe space for emotional processing.

If you feel ready and aligned, you can continue to the next step. However, it is important to honor your intuition and not rush the process. Healing is not a race, and each step and integration holds valuable lessons and insights.

Allow your body to adjust to the energetic shifts that are occurring within you. Embrace the journey and be fully present for each moment of transformation and wholeness.

I encourage you to spend ample time with your fragmented self, exploring the depths of their experiences and emotions. There is valuable information to be gained from these fragments, and it is a profound opportunity to understand how fear has impacted your life. Some individuals have even discovered additional fragments through this process, uncovering the interconnectedness of their experiences. Embrace the uniqueness of your own journey and give yourself the time you need to fully explore and learn from these interactions.

Remember, healing is a deeply personal and individual process. Trust yourself and the wisdom that unfolds within you.

Chapter 10

Step Four
Forgiveness

Forgiving the One Who Hurt You

I cannot stress enough the importance of each step in this healing process. It is crucial to follow each step without skipping any, even if you may initially feel it's unnecessary. Each step serves a purpose and contributes to the effectiveness of the overall healing journey.

One step that requires dedicated time and attention is forgiveness. It is necessary to embark on another journey with the light and return to the familiar scene to practice forgiveness. Take your time with this step, as it holds immense significance. Forgiving the person who has caused you pain and altered the course of your life is essential for closing cycles, healing karmic ties, and releasing attachments that hold you back from raising your frequency further.

As you face the person who has caused you pain, make

eye contact to establish a connection. Utilize the power of your light and love to sincerely say, "I forgive you." This is an opportunity for you to express what lies within your heart. Take your time and express everything that arises within you.

It is important to recognize that true forgiveness goes beyond the need for forgiveness itself. When you are genuinely ready to forgive, you will understand that your soul perceives the pain and story of the other person's soul. These journeys involve your spirit doing the work, not just your conscious mind or limited beliefs. Your soul and spirit possess a deeper understanding and a higher level of consciousness than your physical self. It is remarkable how clients, who were initially convinced they could never forgive their perpetrators, have discovered the capacity for love within themselves through this process.

When you feel ready, embark on another inner journey. Get into a comfortable position, close your eyes, and allow yourself to delve into the depths of your subconscious mind. This time, reconnect with the memory you previously visited and encounter the person who caused you harm. Approach them with patience and mindfulness, observing the details and nuances of the situation. As you progress, you may gain a new perspective and deeper understanding. This exploration may reveal lingering resentment or surprising ease in forgiveness. Remember, the goal is not perfection but to use these journeys as opportunities for learning and profound insights. Through these explorations, you will uncover the workings of your subconscious mind, which significantly impact your life.

When the time is right for forgiveness, you will witness the appearance of another portal of light. This time, it is for the person who has hurt you—the person you have for-

STEP FOUR: FORGIVENESS

*Your soul and spirit possess a
deeper understanding and a higher
level of consciousness than your
physical self.*

given. Invite them to cross the portal, signifying the release of your attachment to them and the event. As they pass through the portal, you can simply experience the healing energy. Afterwards, gently return to your body by wiggling your toes, taking deep breaths, and slowly opening your eyes.

Forgiveness is a powerful tool for freeing ourselves from the grip of trauma and emotional pain. It allows us to release attachments to people and events that have caused us suffering, thereby restoring our personal power. When we hold onto these attachments, they can weaken our boundaries, self-esteem, and confidence. However, by consciously choosing to let go, we reclaim our inner strength and bring it back to ourselves. Forgiveness is a liberating act that empowers us to move forward and create a positive and healthy future.

As we diligently retrieve our fragmented soul parts, we embark on a journey of reclaiming personal power. This transformative process unfolds as we liberate ourselves from the patterns of codependency, freeing ourselves from the reliance on external sources such as people, places, and things to fill our inner void. Through this profound inner work, we reawaken our inner strength and foster an authentic sense of independence, drawing upon the radiance of our own inner light to guide and nurture us. It is through this self-discovery that we come to realize the profound truth: the very essence we desperately sought was residing within us all along, awaiting our recognition and embrace.

Remember, forgiveness is a deeply personal and transformative process. Give yourself the space and time needed to engage in this step fully. Embrace the healing journey and allow the profound energy of forgiveness to flow through you.

STEP FOUR: FORGIVENESS

Every step of the Soul Mending journey is a personal and individual experience, differing from one person to another. I would like to share a couple of client examples that highlight the power of forgiveness, even in the face of initial resistance and uncertainty.

Client #1: During my client's second session, we reached a pivotal moment where the topic of forgiveness arose. However, she expressed strong reluctance due to her difficult past with an abusive uncle. She firmly believed that she wasn't ready to forgive him. I assured her that forgiveness is a personal decision and there was no pressure to force it. True healing comes when the soul is ready.

I encouraged her to connect with the intention of forgiveness and trust her intuition. Together, we embarked on the journey, providing a safe and supportive space for her. As she revisited a significant memory where she had encountered her fragmented self, she noticed the absence of the fragmented part. This confirmed that she had reunited with her inner self and was prepared for the next phase of healing.

In that memory, her uncle stood before her, representing the source of her pain and anger. Almost instantly, she gained insight into his own life story and experiences. She witnessed pivotal moments in his life that had shaped him into the person he had become, including the challenges and hardships he faced. This newfound understanding helped her see that he, too, had been a victim of circumstances beyond his control.

Filled with love and compassion, she gently placed her hand on her uncle's shoulder, assuring him that everything would be okay. In that profound moment, she let go of resentment and embraced forgiveness. A radiant light symbolized a transformative shift in their relationship. She guided her uncle towards the light, symbolizing their mutual release and liberation.

This powerful experience demonstrates the incredible potential of forgiveness to transcend deep wounds and facilitate healing. It highlights the capacity for empathy and understanding as my client recognized the interconnectedness of their stories and the underlying pain that influenced her uncle's actions. Through forgiveness, she reclaimed her personal power and offered him the possibility of redemption.

It is essential to recognize that forgiveness is a personal journey, and each person's readiness and process may differ. My client's courageous act of forgiveness showcases the profound transformation that can occur when we choose to release resentment and embrace compassion.

Client #2: I remember a client who came to me seeking help in healing from a past abusive relationship. Even though she had moved on, the pain still lingered inside her. After successfully bringing back her fragmented self, it was time for her to embark on a journey of forgiveness. She chose to explore a memory in a kitchen where a violent incident had occurred. To her surprise, she found herself face-to-face with her ex-partner, but what caught her off guard was the presence of his mother and sister.

In that profound moment, she engaged in heartfelt conversations with each of them, expressing the deep pain and trauma she had experienced. As she opened her heart to forgiveness, something extraordinary happened. A radiant light appeared for each person she forgave, symbolizing the release of resentment and the restoration of harmony. She discovered that she had carried pain not only from her ex-partner but also from his mother and sister, which was a revelation to her.

This transformative experience became a turning point in her healing journey. It unveiled the layers of pain she had held onto, even towards those indirectly involved in the abusive relationship. By acknowledging and forgiving each person, she reclaimed her power and freed herself from the burdens of resentment and anger.

This journey of forgiveness not only brought deep healing to my client but also taught us a valuable lesson. It revealed the complexities of relationships and how pain and trauma can arise from unexpected sources. Through her courageous act of forgiveness, she not only found solace and liberation but also gained valuable insights into the dynamics that had contributed to her suffering.

Detach: You Are Not Your Trauma

Forgiveness is a transformative process that allows us to detach from past events and release attachments. By forgiving, we free ourselves and rise above lower energies that hinder our growth and expansion. These attachments often hold karmic significance, offering us valuable soul lessons in this lifetime. As we release these attachments and raise our vibration, our frequency begins to shift, bringing about profound changes in our being.

One of the beautiful aspects of healing is that it impacts everyone involved. By engaging in our own healing journey and practicing forgiveness, we bring healing to the person who has caused us pain. It may seem paradoxical to forgive those who have hurt us, but as we progress in our healing, we find love and compassion in our hearts even for those who have wronged us. Through forgiveness, we not only release ourselves but also offer the opportunity for the healing of others. The impact of our healing extends far beyond ourselves, reaching our loved ones and even the collective consciousness. The ripple effect of healing is immense and carries the potential for profound transformation.

In this journey of healing, our relationships, especially with our parents, hold significant karmic weight. These relationships serve as spiritual assistance in our healing process. They are soul contracts designed to facilitate our learning, growth, and expansion. The people who have hurt us are playing their roles in this cosmic play until we learn our lessons and heal from the experiences. If we dismiss these opportunities for growth and healing, we may continue to attract similar situations and people into our lives, even if external circumstances change. These dynamics mirror our inner healing needs and provide us with valuable insights into ourselves. By paying attention and using these opportunities to learn about ourselves, we can shift from victimhood to self-empowerment. It's essential to note that forgiveness does not mean accepting abuse or mistreatment, but rather allows us to transcend victimhood and reclaim our personal power.

Forgiveness holds tremendous power. It is like shedding sandbags from a hot air balloon, allowing us to rise and experience freedom. As we become lighter, we must adjust to new energies and vibrations. Our frequency shifts, and our level of consciousness expands as we leave one realm behind and enter another. Realms can be compared to different floors in a department store, each requiring us to heal, release, and raise our vibration before granting access to the next level. To progress, we must travel light, leaving behind what no longer serves us. This process of

STEP FOUR: FORGIVENESS

Forgiveness holds tremendous power. It is like shedding sandbags from a hot air balloon, allowing us to rise and experience freedom.

adjustment and alignment to new energies is essential as we journey through realms, ascending to higher altitudes and encountering higher frequencies.

During this journey, you may experience sadness and grief as you leave behind people and places energetically, if not physically. It is a natural part of the process. Remember that manifestation occurs not just by thinking about what you want, but by embodying it. Self-forgiveness may also come into play, as you recognize and release any guilt or remorse for past actions or a lack of understanding others' pain. Approach each journey with an open mind and heart, allowing the information and insights to unfold naturally.

If you find it challenging to reach a place of forgiveness, there is no judgment. It simply means that more healing needs to occur, and it will happen when you are ready. Avoid rushing or forcing the process, as it requires completing each step and expanding your awareness along the way. The healing journey is not about achieving something or obtaining external validation; it is about gaining clarity, knowledge, and expanding consciousness. The most valuable information you will encounter comes from within during your inner journey. Embrace the process and the lessons it brings, rather than focusing solely on completion or success. There is no finish line, no certificate or diploma to obtain. Real freedom lies in releasing attachments, shedding the armor and masks that have concealed our pain and wounds.

Embarking on a spiritual healing journey can feel lonely at times. It is beneficial to surround yourself with a supportive community that can hold space for you throughout your healing process. While you alone must do the inner work, having a support system can provide comfort, encouragement, and guidance. As your energy shifts and you undergo profound internal changes, your outer reality will naturally align with your inner world. This is how energy operates. You may attract new people into your life who are energetically aligned with where you are on your journey, providing further support and understanding.

Embrace the power of forgiveness, the transformative nature of healing, and the journey itself. Allow yourself to be supported and guided as you navigate this profound process of self-discovery and growth. Remember, the path of healing is unique to everyone, and it unfolds in its own time. Trust in the process and honor your own journey as you move towards greater wholeness and liberation.

Chapter 11

Step Five
Gratitude

Connecting to Your Light

The final step of gratitude in the healing process is beautiful and powerful. It involves connecting with the light that resides within you, the essence of your being. This light exists in your heart and is the source of love and connection to all living things. It is a divine spark, a fragment of the infinite source energy from which you originated.

As beings of light, our true nature is one of love and purity. Light carries a higher frequency than darker energies, which can impact our overall well-being. By cultivating gratitude, we amplify and expand this inner light. Gratitude acts as a booster, enhancing our connection to the light within us. Take a moment to close your eyes, visualize a bright light within your chest, and focus on it. Feel its energy and vibration, bathing in its presence. Allow it to grow and expand infinitely.

Where our attention goes, energy flows. If we focus on darkness and fear, they too grow. However, as we continue to heal and release lower vibrational energies, our inner light becomes more prominent. The light is our true essence, the energy we are born from—an all-loving energy source. By reconnecting with this light, we reconnect with ourselves. Even if you don't feel the light within you or perceive it as dim, it is always there. The fact that you are alive is proof of its existence. You are never too far from home, from your inner light.

Imagine a glass bowl filled with pure, clear water. Now, imagine a drop of black ink falling into the bowl. Gradually, more drops follow, darkening the water. Despite the darkness, the fact remains that there is still water in the bowl. Your spirit, your light, is like that water. The black ink represents the fear that taints your energy, bit by bit. It may feel like things are dark, and heavy energy may weigh you down, but your light is always present, unextinguished. The key is to dive deep into the bowl of water and confront each particle of black ink. Acknowledge it and transform it. Though it may seem challenging, you have the power to transform the energy, releasing fear and embracing love. It requires dedication and courage, qualities that you possess.

When we sit in gratitude, we begin to see events as opportunities for growth and learning. By practicing gratitude for the light within us, we can even extend gratitude to those who have caused us pain. Gratitude brings meaning to our lives and helps us understand the purpose behind our experiences. We recognize the important contracts we have with the people in our lives, as we support each other's learning, growth, healing, and expansion.

Gratitude is not only the final step in the healing process but also a practice that can be incorporated daily. It

STEP FIVE: GRATITUDE

magnifies your inner light, intensifies your experiences, and shifts your perspective. Embrace the transformative power of gratitude as you continue your healing journey, allowing your light to shine ever brighter.

Chapter 12

The Summary

Let's have a quick recap of the Soul Mending steps:

1. *Starting Point*: Choose a starting point, such as an emotion, trigger, or physical pain, and frame it as a question. Remember, a question brings direction so have your question in your mind before starting on your journey. Pay close attention to your triggers as they provide a clear direction for your healing journey. In my experience, triggers act as a readily available and noticeable starting point for our healing process. They often appear in our everyday lives, giving us many chances to explore and become more self-aware. To begin this journey, take the time to consciously observe your triggers throughout your day. Pay attention to them and make a note of them.

2. *The Discovery*: Journey within to connect with a

fragmented soul part. Allow yourself to explore without control, using your senses to see, feel, and know the information you receive. Spend time here to gain deeper insight into the event and the extent of your emotional wound. It is important to keep an open mind because you might discover your fragment in the most unexpected of places.

3. *Going Home*: Regain the trust of the fragmented soul part and invite it back into your body, which it left due to the pain. Look for a portal of light and walk through it hand in hand with your past self, bringing the fragmented part back home. Remember, the process of bringing your fragment home may require multiple journeys, and it is important to honor the time it takes for both you and your fragment to be ready for the reunion.

4. *Forgiveness*: Return to the same place with the intention to offer forgiveness to the person who caused you pain. Trust your intuition and keep an open mind. When forgiveness occurs, a portal of light will appear, inviting the person to walk through it. This releases you from the attachment to the person and the event. Even when you feel unable to forgive, embark on the journey with the intention of forgiveness and remain open to what unfolds. Trust in your intuition and soul, as they comprehend things that may elude your conscious self.

5. *Gratitude*: Cultivate gratitude for your own light. While gratitude can also be extended to the people and things in your life, it is essential to acknowledge and appreciate the light within yourself. It is through this inner light that you can bring healing to the world.

THE SUMMARY

By embracing these steps, you embark on a profound and transformative journey of healing, aimed at mending your soul and rediscovering your authentic essence. Although they may appear simple, trust that they hold the potential to bring profound changes to your life. As you engage in this process, you will begin by asking a question or setting an intention, allowing your subconscious to guide you to relevant events or memories. It is important to remain open and curious, as this journey may lead you to unexpected places and unveil connections that you may not have initially imagined. This is precisely the purpose of the process—to transcend the limitations of the conscious mind and tap into the depths of intuition and subconscious wisdom. Through this exploration, you will uncover the hidden links between past traumas and your current life situation, gaining a deeper understanding of the underlying root causes and their impact on your present experience.

Healing in Two Parts

By consciously breaking down the comprehensive healing process into two distinct parts, individuals can embark on a purposeful and gradual journey towards healing. The first part involves actively exploring and connecting with fragmented soul parts, as well as integrating and assimilating the retrieved aspects into one's being. This process allows for a deepening of self-awareness and a profound transformation to take place over time. The second part focuses on releasing oneself from the attachments and shackles of the pain and trauma, liberating the soul from their grip and allowing for a sense of freedom and inner peace to emerge. Through this approach, individuals can experience a more harmonious and sustainable healing process, nurturing their overall well-being and facilitating a profound shift in their lives.

Here's a breakdown of the two parts:

Part 1: The Initiation

Step 1: Embark on a journey of self-discovery and connection with your fragmented part: Now is the moment to begin a journey within yourself, delving into the hidden parts of your subconscious mind to discover the origins of trauma and fear. As you encounter the wounded aspect, engage in a meaningful interaction with a particular memory or event. Dedicate sufficient time to establish a deep and heartfelt connection with your inner child or younger self. Adopt the role of a nurturing and understanding caregiver, offering the love and support that may have been missing in the past. Embrace this chance to explore the depths of this connection, unveiling valuable information and gaining profound insights throughout the process.

Step 2: Prepare for the process of reintegration: Dedicate sufficient time and attention to understanding the needs and emotions of your fragmented part. Embrace the opportunity to perceive your personal history through a fresh lens, gaining new insights and understanding. Uncover hidden facets of their personality that may have become lost or inaccessible to you, as you navigate the path towards wholeness and integration. Allow this transformative journey to unfold at its own pace, fostering a deeper connection and harmonious reunion with your fragmented part.

Step 3: Extend a heartfelt invitation for their homecoming:

When you feel a sense of readiness within, softly inquire if your fragmented part is also prepared to begin the journey of reintegration into your being. If their willingness aligns, gently guide them through the portal of light, warmly inviting them back into the sacred space of your heart. Recognize that this precious fragment may need gentle healing and deliberate integration and respect the importance of granting sufficient time for this deep process of transformation to unfold naturally and harmoniously.

Part 2: The Completion

Step 4: Dive into the exploration of forgiveness: Return to the familiar space where you initially connected with your fragmented part and embark on a journey of forgiveness. Pause for a moment to consider if there are individuals, including yourself, who could benefit from your compassionate forgiveness. Fully immerse yourself in this sacred environment, granting yourself the freedom to ask questions, express genuine emotions, and cultivate space for personal growth and deep comprehension to blossom.

Step 5: Cultivate gratitude and embrace your radiant light: After you have embraced the transformative act of forgiveness, take a moment to immerse yourself in the radiant energy of gratitude for the light within you. Find a cozy place to sit or lay down and reflect on the remarkable growth and blossoming of your inner light throughout this healing journey. Notice the vivid hue and vibrant energy it radiates, acknowledging and cherishing the remarkable strides you have made. Let gratitude overflow from your heart as you embrace the profound beauty and resilience that emanate from the depths of your being.

After completing these steps, how can you recognize your healing progress? A significant sign of healing can be observed in your interactions with others, particularly if the person who caused you pain continues to be a part of your life and you feel safe in their presence. During these encounters, carefully observe your experiences and emotions. Notice any changes in their energy, your ability to remain less affected by their words and actions, and the development of stronger personal boundaries. These interactions can provide valuable insights and act as a measure of your progress along the path of healing.

It is crucial to remember that healing is a highly individual and unique journey, and the amount of time and integration required may vary from person to person. Trust your inner wisdom and grant yourself the necessary space and patience for the healing process to unfold in its entirety. Respect and uphold your boundaries and ensure that you only engage in situations and environments where you feel genuinely comfortable and safe.

It is essential to prioritize your well-being and honor your personal limits. By doing so, you create a supportive and nurturing space for your healing journey, allowing for continued growth, empowerment, and self-care. Remember, you have the right to set boundaries that serve your highest good and protect your emotional and physical well-being.

Grounding Yourself

As you embark on your energetic healing journey, it is important to maintain a sense of grounding. Grounding acts as an anchor, providing stability and focus throughout the process, preventing you from feeling destabilized. Just like a building needs a solid foundation to stand tall, your energetic body and chakras also require a stable base to support their shifting and adjustment.

Remaining grounded means staying connected to the present moment and to the Earth's energy. Remember, the earth element is associated with the root chakra, your base and foundation. Grounding involves finding practices that help you stay rooted and centered, even when faced with the challenges and transformations that come with healing.

Here is a list of practices that can support you in getting and maintaining a grounded state. While exploring these techniques, feel free to integrate those that deeply resonate with you and align with your unique journey:

1. *Mindfulness Meditation*: Engage in regular mindfulness meditation sessions, focusing your attention on the present moment, observing your thoughts and sensations without judgment. This practice helps cultivate a sense of grounding and presence.

2. *Body Awareness*: Tune into your body by practicing body scan exercises. Start from the top of your head and gradually move down, paying attention to each body part, noticing any sensations, and bringing your awareness to the physical sensations of grounding, such as the contact of your feet with the ground.

3. *Grounding Visualizations*: Imagine roots extending from the soles of your feet or the base of your spine, anchoring you deep into the earth. Visualize these roots growing and intertwining with the earth's core, providing you with stability and a sense of being grounded.

4. *Engage in Physical Activity*: Participate in activities that involve physical movement, such as walking, running, yoga, or dancing. These exercises not only promote physical well-being but also help to ground your energy and release any accumulated tension.
5. *Connect with Earth Elements*: Embrace the elements of nature, such as earth, water, air, and fire. Spend time near bodies of water, sit by a bonfire, or immerse yourself in the healing energy of the earth by gardening or simply sitting on the ground.
6. *Use Grounding Crystals*: Carry or wear grounding crystals such as hematite, smoky quartz, black tourmaline, or jasper. These crystals are believed to have grounding properties and can assist in stabilizing your energy.
7. *Practice Earthing*: Spend time barefoot on the earth, whether it's walking on grass, sand, or soil. Allow the earth's energy to flow through you, revitalizing your energy and grounding your being.
8. *Engage in Creative Expression*: Explore artistic activities such as painting, drawing, writing, or playing an instrument. These forms of self-expression can help you connect with your inner self and bring about a sense of grounding.
9. *Cultivate Gratitude*: Regularly express gratitude for the blessings and abundance in your life. This practice helps shift your focus to the present moment and cultivates a sense of grounding by acknowledging and appreciating what you have
10. *Set Boundaries*: Honor your personal boundaries

and communicate your needs and limits. By setting healthy boundaries, you create a safe and secure space for yourself, fostering a sense of grounding and self-empowerment.

Remember, grounding is an ongoing practice, and it may require regular attention and exploration to find the techniques that work best for you. Allow yourself the freedom to experiment and adapt these practices to suit your unique needs and preferences.

The Healing Crisis

The healing crisis, also known as the "healing reaction" or "detoxification reaction," is an integral part of the healing journey. It refers to a temporary period of discomfort or intensification of symptoms that can occur as the body, mind, and spirit undergo a transformative healing process. During this phase, the body releases stored toxins, emotions, and energetic blockages, allowing for deep healing and the shedding of old beliefs and energies that no longer serve us.

It's important to understand that the healing crisis is a natural response and indicates that the body is actively working to restore balance and promote well-being. While it can be uncomfortable, it is a sign of progress on the healing path. It may manifest as physical symptoms, emotional ups and downs, or a temporary increase in stress levels. These experiences may vary for each individual and depend on the nature of the healing process and the specific areas being addressed.

This process can be uncomfortable, but it is a natural

part of healing and shedding old beliefs and energies that no longer serve us. During a healing crisis, you may experience emotional and physical symptoms as your energy shifts and your frequency increases. These symptoms can vary from burning chest sensations and existential questions to a sense of loss and a shift in the significance of outside influences in your life. It's important to remember that these symptoms are normal and are indicators of your soul healing and ascending to a higher level of consciousness.

You may also experience ascension symptoms such as pressure on the chest or upper back, ringing in the ears, and sensitivity at the top of the head. These symptoms are unique to each individual and can serve as reminders of the ongoing healing and transformation process. Grounding yourself and allowing the energies to settle and integrate is crucial during this time.

It's understandable to feel alarmed or lose faith in the healing process when experiencing discomfort and the surfacing of old beliefs and thoughts. However, it's important to trust the process and refrain from interfering with it. The energies are reaching their climax and releasing, and interfering may disrupt the natural flow of healing. It's a time to stay connected and feel everything, finding comfort in the discomfort and recognizing the growth and expansion that occur through these experiences.

It's crucial to approach the healing crisis with patience, self-compassion, and support. Here are some strategies to navigate through this phase:

1. *Self-Care*: Prioritize self-care practices that nourish and support your overall well-being. This can include getting adequate rest, eating nutritious foods, staying hydrated, and engaging in activities that bring you joy

and relaxation.

2. *Emotional Release*: Allow yourself to express and release emotions that come up during the healing crisis. This can be done through journaling, talking with a trusted friend or therapist, or engaging in creative outlets such as art or music.

3. *Mindfulness and Acceptance*: Practice mindfulness to cultivate present-moment awareness and acceptance of what comes up during the healing process. Embrace the discomfort as a natural part of transformation and remind yourself that it is temporary.

4. *Seek Support*: Reach out to a supportive community, therapist, or healer who can provide guidance, validation, and assistance during this phase. Having someone to lean on can offer comfort and reassurance as you navigate through the healing crisis.

5. *Trust the Process*: Have faith in your body's innate wisdom and trust that the healing crisis is a necessary step towards greater well-being. Trusting the process allows you to surrender to the journey and open yourself to the transformative power of healing.

The healing crisis is a testament to your commitment to growth and self-care. Embracing this phase with patience and self-compassion will ultimately lead to a deeper level of healing, liberation, and alignment with your authentic self.

The Expansion

Releasing fear is a transformative process that allows you to expand and express your true essence. Fear has a way of keeping us small and limiting our possibilities. By letting go of fear, you can tap into your infinite potential and experience a greater sense of freedom.

When starting a new project or endeavor, fear may arise, indicating that there are underlying fears that need to be healed. Pay attention to your emotions and any feelings of being blocked, annoyed, or stressed during the process. These emotions can serve as clues to uncovering and healing deeper fears. Awareness is key, as we can only heal what we are aware of.

The healing process is not always linear, and memories or emotions may surface in unexpected ways. Stay open and flexible, trusting in the process and following your intuition. Healing happens at your own pace and in alignment with your highest good.

Releasing fears and attachments is essential for your soul's growth, expansion, and ascension. These fears hold you back from raising your vibration and experiencing transformation. As you recalibrate your energy and make profound changes, you not only impact your own life but also have a ripple effect on your ancestors and future generations. It has the potential to heal generational traumas and create positive shifts for your family and those connected to you.

On a collective level, our mission is to co-create a harmonious and joyful existence on Earth. We are all here, consciously, or unconsciously, working on our healing and raising the vibration of the planet. By releasing fear and aligning with love, compassion, and openness, we can collectively create a world where pain, struggle, and sacrifice are no longer the norm. Abundance and harmony are available to us, and it's a matter of aligning ourselves to fully receive and embody these blessings.

Conclusion

In your healing journey, it is important to recognize that you are never alone. There is a vast network of spiritual beings, guides, and guardian angels who are available to assist and support you. These entities are present to offer guidance, wisdom, and comfort as you navigate your healing process. One powerful connection you can establish is with your higher self, the divine aspect of your being that is always present and guiding you. Even if you do not perceive or feel the presence of your higher self at this moment, you can utilize the power of your imagination to forge a connection. Allow yourself to enter a realm of imagination, where you can dream, envision, and transcend into another world where you can meet and connect with your higher self.

If you currently do not have a specific helping spirit to connect with, simply invite the light to accompany you on your healing journey. Request its presence and guidance as you delve into your healing work. It is beneficial to engage in this transformative process when you are well-rested, in a positive state of mind, and attuned to the energy of the light. By doing so, you create a conducive environment for a more uplifting and empowering healing experience. If you encounter moments where you feel stuck or unable to find clear answers, it is crucial to bring yourself back to the present moment and ground yourself in the here and now.

It is essential to remember that this healing process is

not about performance or achieving immediate results. It is a journey of introspection, self-discovery, and healing. It serves as a reminder that you possess the innate ability to heal yourself. The focus lies in the profound changes you can initiate within yourself and the growth and expansion you can experience. There is no predetermined finish line or race to complete. Healing is an ongoing and continuous process because your potential for growth and transformation is limitless. You will continue to evolve, expand, and heal in the spiritual realm and future lifetimes. You do not need to accomplish everything before departing from this physical existence. Embrace the understanding that healing is an eternal and ever-unfolding journey.

As you embrace your healing journey, remember to be gentle and patient with yourself. Give yourself permission to experience the emotions and challenges that arise, knowing that they are integral parts of your healing process. Allow yourself to receive the support and guidance from the spiritual realm, your higher self, and the beings that are ready to assist you. Trust in your own inner wisdom and intuition as you navigate the twists and turns of your healing path.

In your interactions with the spiritual realm, it is important to cultivate a sense of openness, receptivity, and gratitude. Express your gratitude for the assistance and healing that flows into your life. Cultivate a sense of awe and wonder for the interconnectedness of all beings and the infinite possibilities that lie within you.

Through your healing journey, may you find solace, strength, and transformation. May you embrace the interconnectedness of all aspects of your being and the guidance of the spiritual realm. May you remember that healing is a profound and eternal process, and you have the power to create positive change within yourself and the world around you.

Final Thoughts

As you delve deeper into the process of Soul Mending, you will discover that you have the innate ability to read and understand energy. You become an intuitive energy reader, accessing your own energy field to gather information and transform your energy. This realization empowers you and reveals the immense power you possess.

Through Soul Mending, you begin to live more from your heart space, allowing your heart to guide you instead of relying solely on your mind. With the release of fear and the healing of trauma, your mind can now find a new purpose and become a valuable tool in your self-expression. Freed from the burden of constant defense, your mind can redirect its energy towards creative endeavors, self-reflection, and self-discovery. It can support you in exploring your passions, pursuing your goals, and expressing your unique gifts and talents.

As your mind rests from its previous defensive role, it becomes more receptive to new experiences, perspectives, and possibilities. It can engage in open-mindedness, curiosity, and exploration, allowing you to expand your awareness and deepen your understanding of yourself and the world around you. Your mind becomes a powerful instrument for learning, growth, and self-empowerment.

With a mind that is no longer overwhelmed by fear-based thoughts and limiting beliefs, you can cultivate a greater sense of presence and mindfulness. You can fully engage in the present moment, free from excessive worry or anxiety about the past or future. This presence enables you to connect more deeply with yourself and others, enhancing your relationships and fostering a greater sense of connection and belonging.

By utilizing your mind as a tool for self-expression, you can effectively communicate your thoughts, emotions, and desires to the world. You can express your creativity, share your ideas, and engage in meaningful conversations and interactions. Your mind becomes a vehicle for authentic self-expression and a means to contribute to the collective consciousness.

By opening your heart, you create a powerful shift within yourself that extends far beyond your personal healing. Opening your heart allows you to connect with others on a deeper level and cultivate meaningful relationships. It is through these connections that you can experience a greater sense of love, belonging, and support.

When you open your heart, you let go of emotional barriers and walls that may have been erected because of past hurts and traumas. This vulnerability and openness create a safe space for genuine connections to form. You become more receptive to giving and receiving love, compassion, and understanding.

As you release fear and heal trauma, your heart expands, enabling you to experience a profound sense of empathy and compassion towards yourself and others. You develop a greater capacity for understanding and accepting the diverse experiences and emotions of those around you. This empathy deepens your connections and fosters a sense of unity and interconnectedness.

Opening your heart allows you to tap into the abundant flow of love and blessings that are available to you. When your heart is open, you become aligned with the frequency of love, which attracts positive experiences and opportunities into your life. You become a magnet for love, joy, and abundance.

Opening your heart also plays a significant role in your spiritual expansion. Spirituality is not confined to religious beliefs but encompasses a broader understanding of your connection to something greater than yourself. When your heart is open, you align with the essence of your true self and the higher realms of consciousness.

Through this alignment, you gain access to higher wisdom, intuition, and spiritual insights. You begin to perceive life through the lens of love and interconnectedness, recognizing the divine presence within yourself and others. This spiritual expansion brings a sense of purpose, fulfillment, and alignment with your soul's journey.

The healing journey is a remarkable and transformative process that unfolds with numerous wonderful and unexpected outcomes. As you embark on your personal healing journey, you may experience remarkable shifts in your perception and connection to the unseen realms. During the process of healing, the energetic barriers and limitations that may have hindered the expression of your spiritual gifts can gradually dissolve, revealing innate abilities like clairvoyance, clairaudience, clairsentience, and claircognizance.

Clairvoyance, which involves seeing beyond the physical world, may become more vivid and clear as your energetic pathways open and align. You might start receiving meaningful visual impressions, symbols, or images that carry deeper insights and significance.

Clairaudience, the ability to hear messages from the spiritual realm, may be amplified, allowing you to receive guidance and wisdom through subtle whispers, inner voices, or even external sounds that carry profound meaning.

Clairsentience, the ability to sense and feel energy, emotions, and vibrations, may become more heightened. This enables you to intuitively perceive the energetic essence of people, places, and situations, providing valuable information and guidance.

Claircognizance, the ability to know information beyond logical reasoning, may strengthen, granting you a deep sense of inner knowing and clarity. Insights and understanding may arise within you without a rational explanation.

These spiritual abilities serve as powerful tools for self-discovery, guidance, and connecting with the spiritual realm. Embracing and developing these gifts can enhance your spiritual growth, deepen your connection with higher consciousness, and offer profound insights into your own healing journey and the world around you. It is important to approach the development of these abilities with an open mind, mindfulness, and a commitment to personal growth, allowing them to unfold naturally and align with your highest good.

Trust plays a significant role in this process. Trust the information you receive through your senses—images, thoughts, sounds, and physical sensations. Trust is essential, and with an open heart, you can surrender to the healing process and its transformative effects.

Remember, this book is a reminder of your innate abilities as a healer and energy reader. You brought these skills and knowledge from the spiritual realm into the physical world. Just as you carry your previous experiences and skills into a new job, you can apply your spiritual abilities here on Earth.

Soul Mending is an ongoing process that deepens your intuition and invites you to explore your inner world. As you become more comfortable with the journey within, you'll find that your intuition becomes stronger, and you can access answers more readily. Allow your intuition to guide your healing process and follow the promptings of your heart.

In time, you will notice the speed and ease with which you can engage in this process. When emotions arise, you will reflexively dive deeper into self-inquiry, focusing on the root causes rather than the surface-level reactions. This expanded perspective and heightened awareness contribute to your overall consciousness.

You will begin to feel lighter, more present, and aligned as you continue with soul mending. Life will be experienced with more love and lightness in your heart. However, you may also encounter tests—situations that offer you the opportunity to respond differently than you would have in the past. These tests allow you to gauge your energetic shifts and the healing you have undergone.

Be patient with yourself as you embark on this journey. Over time, you will witness the profound transformation and experience the wholeness and alignment of your being. Embrace the limitless possibilities that your imagination presents and allow your soul to guide you toward healing and expansion.

Where to Go from Here

I understand that embarking on a healing journey can be challenging, and it's important to remember to be kind and compassionate towards yourself throughout the process. Healing involves shifting energies and adjusting both mentally and physically, which can be tiring. So, please take the time to rest and nurture yourself whenever you feel the need.

It's crucial not to rush or pressure yourself to heal quickly or achieve perfection. Healing is an ongoing, lifelong process that extends beyond our time on Earth. So, be patient and gentle with yourself as you navigate this transformative path.

Going at it alone can be challenging so I created a Soul Mending community, a sanctuary where healing, growth, and transformation are nurtured with kindness and compassion. We are here to support you on your journey of self-discovery and soulful healing.

In this community, we understand the significance of self-care and the importance of embracing our authentic selves. We recognize that healing can be a profound and sometimes exhausting process, requiring patience, understanding, and a gentle approach. With that in mind, we have created a space where you can find solace, guidance, and the resources you need to navigate your own unique healing journey.

Our commitment to your well-being extends beyond words. We have curated a collection of meditations, including the powerful Heart Activation Meditation and chakra healing meditations, to assist you in accessing your inner wisdom and restoring balance to your energetic being. These meditations are designed to accompany you as you delve into the depths of your soul, allowing for healing and transformation to unfold at a pace that feels right for you.

To further support you, we offer the Soul Mending Pod, a series of videos and online sessions where you can experience the healing energy and guidance that have touched the lives of many before you. These sessions provide a safe and nurturing space for you to explore the depths of your being, connect with your intuition, and embrace your innate healing abilities.

But our community is not just about individual healing. It is also a place where we come together, forming a collective of souls united in our shared journeys. Through online healing events, workshops, healing circles, and retreats, we foster connections and create opportunities for growth, learning, and profound healing experiences. In this community, you will find a supportive network of individuals who understand the challenges and triumphs of the healing process and are ready to walk alongside you every step of the way.

I invite you to visit soulmending.ca, where you can learn more about our upcoming events and offerings. Join us on this transformative path, and together, let us discover the infinite possibilities of healing, self-discovery, and personal empowerment. You are not alone on this journey — we are here to uplift, inspire, and support you as you embark on the beautiful adventure of Soul Mending.

www.ingramcontent.com/pod-product-compliance
Lightning Source LLC
Chambersburg PA
CBHW031115080526
44587CB00011B/983